RING OF BONE

RING OF BONE

Collected Poems of Lew Welch

Edited by Donald Allen

With a Foreword by Gary Snyder

CITY LIGHTS / GREY FOX
San Francisco

Cover photograph of Lew Welch, 1965 by Steamboat,
   aka Jim Hatch
Cover design by Linda Ronan

Library of Congress Cataloging-in-Publication Data

Welch, Lew.
Ring of bone : collected poems of Lew Welch / edited by Donald
Allen ; with a foreword by Gary Snyder. — New & expanded ed.
p. cm.
Includes bibliographical references.
ISBN 978-0-87286-579-2
1. Beat generation—Poetry. I. Allen, Donald, 1912-2004. II.
Title.

PS3573.E45R5 2012
811'.54—dc23

                    2012012591

City Lights Books are published at the City Lights Bookstore
261 Columbus Avenue, San Francisco, CA 94133
www.citylights.com

To the memory of

Gertrude Stein & William Carlos Williams

I WANT THE WHOLE THING, the moment
when what we thought was rock, or
sea
became clear Mind, and

what we thought was clearest Mind really
was that glancing girl, that
swirl of birds. . .

(all of that)

AND AT THE SAME TIME that very poem
pasted in the florist's window

(as Whalen's I *wanted to bring you this Jap Iris* was)

carefully retyped and
put right out there on Divisadero St.

just because the florist thought it
pretty,

that it might remind of love,
that it might sell flowers . . .

The line

Tangled in Samsara!

Mt. Tamalpais 1970

CONTENTS

Book II (1960-1964) *HERMIT POEMS*

Book III (1960-1964) *THE WAY BACK*

FOREWORD

It will soon be half a century since Lew Welch left his car and his camp and his plans, and walked off into the wilds of the northern Sierra. This book of his poems, *Ring of Bone*, was first published soon after. He was 45 years old then.

Lew was a handsome, talented, and charismatic man who spoke eloquently on many topics — a humanist by education, whose first prose writings were on Gertrude Stein. He was one of a set of four poets in the late '40s who were students at Reed college together — Philip Whalen, Lew, and Gary Snyder the experimentalists, and Wiliam Dickey the brilliant formalist. Whalen, Snyder, and Welch re-grouped in the Bay Area in the late fifties and participated in the San Francisco Renaissance/Beat literary scene.

Don Allen and his Four Seasons Press inherited Lew's literary archive, and published or republished eight books and chapbooks by Lew. *Ring of Bone* is the major volume of poems, and since the smaller "Selected" is long out of print, I will quote some of the Preface I wrote then:

> What we recognize as poetry, different from rock lyrics
> say, carries a large body of cultural and archetypal lore
> ("makings") in loops from the past, also aiming into the
> future. The Poems in *Ring of Bone* have an underlying
> drone-tone, like the tamboura of Indian music: a rich
> basic Asian and Occidental humane grounding.
>
> Lew Welch writes lyrical poems of clarity, humor,
> and dark probings. The poems brought together in
> this selection are the major works of a man who of his
> forty-five years of life in the west gave twenty-one to
> poetry. His work stands in the context of San Francisco
> poetry renaissance: the post-World War II libertarian
> energy of striving to further develop the possibilities of
> open-form poetry. The heart of the book is the "Hermit
> Poems" and "Way Back" sections — poems evoking,
> covering, the time spent in retreat and practice at a
> cabin in the mountains of coast north California deep
> up rivers still Yurok land. In those works Lew achieved
> the meeting of an ancient sage tradition and the "shack
> simple" post frontier back country of out-of-work work-
> ingman's style, and then the (elite) rebel modernism of

art He returned to the Bay Area at the inception of the over-heavy flowering of hippie culture. It is instructive how these poems have the essence but cut through the psychedelic baroque.

The title *Ring of Bone* comes from one of his poems. It was written we are told in 1963 when he was living and writing in that cabin tucked away up a canyon on the Salmon river — pulling together lines and thoughts from a letter to Robert Duncan that was never sent. It is part of the "Hermit Poem" series.

As for poetics, jazz musical phrasing of American speech is one of Lew Welch's clearest contributions. First clued in to write in natural speech and in terms of the musical phrase by Williams and Pound, he turns sometimes to street-talk, street-jive, blues, bop rhythms, and can score it on the page. This is done without cuteness or obscurity. Indeed, all these poems have *music* and *clarity* of language and a compression such that "the words stop, but the meaning keeps going on." His reading of Chinese poetry and Japanese haiku in translation sharpened eye and ear, but led to imitation only when in fun.
	Behind, and informing the playfuness and skill of these poems is the evolving consciousness of a man who struggled to be on the Way. He is one of the few who saw the beauty of that ecstatic Mutual Offering called the Food Chain.

(My late wife Carole Koda once said that the "Basic Practice" of her Jodo-shin sect Buddhist upbringing — the school of Buddhism which astutely critiques the "effort" of Yogins and Yoginis and Zen type ascetics to improve themselves — was Church Potlucks.) But Lew was finally brought down by his addiction to alcohol. He and I worked on his addiction together one time, both taking LSD and sitting at the edge of the ridgetop above the hamlet of Stinson Beach. That's where he first really saw the vultures and called them to himself, but then said — almost in despair — "I'm not edible." I was off in my own study of a dancing blinding baby Krishna and then I discovered my sense of smell. We didn't solve Lew's drinking problem, but after that day I never smoked tobacco again.

Poets learn a lot from witches; living with the image of the Teeth Mother was the darker side of Lew's songs. He not only drank too much, he had a way with guns, and took one with him into the woods, never to be seen again, in May of 1971 This is predicted in one of his last pieces, "Song of the Turkey Buzzard."

Lew's memory and mystery lives on. In the spring of 2011 the Central Library of Los Angeles sponsored a gathering of several poets and writers who had known Lew, and we were all surprised by the size and enthusiasm of the crowd that came, people of all ages. City Lights Books took over Lew's works after Donald Allen's death, and in 2011 all of Lew's books were out of print. The Los Angeles celebration of his work was push enough to get us to a new edition of *Ring of Bone*. This bright-eyed bardic spirit, Lew Welch still wandering and singing on the back roads — I imagine — at the far edge of the West — will be with us a long time. As Lew also wrote,

> Guard the Mysteries!
> Constantly reveal Them!

Mystery: the life of art (though poets are always complaining) is without equal. There is nothing to regret.

Gary Snyder, 2012

PREFACE

I. *The Structure*

This book is organized into a structure composed of individual poems, where the poems act somewhat like chapters in a novel. The poems are autobiographical lyrics and the way they are linked together tells a story. Though any of the poems will stand perfectly well by itself, each nourishes and is enriched by the poems before and after it.

I first became struck by the usefulness of such a form through a close study of Yeats' *The Tower*. In that book Yeats addresses himself to the problem of accepting old age, and discusses the subject through short lyric poems some of which cannot be understood without considering the book's scheme, and all of which become larger because of their context. *Les Fleurs du Mal* is another example of such a book, as is *Songs of Innocence and Experience*.

Ring of Bone might be called a spiritual autobiography arranged in more or less chronological sequence. But this does not always mean that poems near the beginning were written first. The mind grows in a flickering kind of way. Sometimes an insight comes too early to be fully understood. At other times, we are shocked that it came, being so obvious, so late. I have also written new poems for the purpose of filling gaps in the story, so any poem may have been written at any time or not. Yeats followed this practice. "Sailing to Byzantium" was written for *The Tower*. It appears first, as a preface so to speak, but it was written in 1927 while later poems were made as early as 1919. The last poem in his book is dated 1920, but resolves the predicament expressed seven years later.

The shape of *Ring of Bone* is circular, or back and forth. Naturally such a form never ends. The principal characters are The Mountain, The City, and The Man who attempts to understand and live with them. The Man changes more than The Mountain and The City, and it appears he will always need both.

The last section, "The Songs Mt. Tamalpais Sings," includes a sampler of the new poems which will make up my next book. It just keeps rolling along.

I'm back on the Mountain.

II. *The Music*

This book is a book of scores, for the voice. The scores will become poems only while they are sounded, performed, sung. Of course. Nobody would dream of calling the little black notes on the page the music of Bach, and so it is with poetry. Some argue that if this is so we ought to publish our poetry on tapes and records only. I don't agree with that at all.

I like the idea of giving my readers a text they can actively perform, themselves. Far too many of our pleasures are spectator sports already. All that is needed is to hear any poet read from his works once or twice. From then on you have an accurate guide to imitate or take liberties with. 1 was never able to enjoy or even read Dylan Thomas until I heard a record of his. From then on his poems were as accessible as conversation. But I wouldn't want to hear all of his work on record, I enjoy doing it myself.

III.

In 1959, I said, in a program note: "When I write my only concern is accuracy. I try to write accurately from the poise of mind which lets us see that things are exactly what they seem. I never worry about beauty, if it is accurate there is always beauty. I never worry about form, if it is accurate there is always form."

I phoned that statement from work. I had a dreary, underpaid job for the Bemis Bag factory, and the roar of their presses and bag-machinery was almost too loud to think, or talk over.

Since 1959 all kinds of things have happened to me and the world, but I still hold to this statement, absolutely.

What was then the "Beat Generation" is now down to a few survivors, each of whom went his only way. Most of us are gone (as so many makers go early) into prisons, looney bins, penthouses, graves, and the other silences of whatever desperation.

It has been no different for us than for any generation. Witness Rexroth's poem on the death of Dylan Thomas, where he lists the victims he loved, who lost. Then counter this, or any other, with the list of poets, painters, dancers, musicians, who lived beyond their fortieth year.

Happily, I'm still alive and am over 40. From such a rare height it is possible to say (in defense of my work, and others here or gone), that today, foolish as they may appear to the frightened eye, young America swings much harder than we did, with less fear, and more love.

American poetry, for at least 50 years, has had to screech above the din of a Bemis Bag. Hart Crane's daddy wanted him to manage the family candy factory. Whitman could say it was marvelous to see the muscled workers. But the poets who followed him (who had to be those workers, at jobs) know that there ain't no muscled workers, they's only victims.

Whitman, the roaming spectator, was victimized later. Fancy professors do it, daily, in the state universities. There's a Walt Whitman Savings and Loan in his old home town. It only goes to show what the reward is, if you work real hard and never cheat.

The sound we hear from our tribe is not much different from the thousand sparrows who used to sleep in a palm tree outside my window, once. The racket was unbelievable, but the birds were only arguing about who has the right to sleep, and where.

So, in my poetry, I've tried to keep the din while still being accurate to the poise of mind that lets us know what's what. Sometimes I've called this din "Letting America speak for itself." Often it's a depressing job.

But I still have faith that if I do this right, accurately, the sound will emerge a "meaningless din of joy." Because I know that the true sound of living things, a carrot or a tribe, is meaningless, joyful, and we, singing it, know this joy.

This sound, the din of joy, is quite distinct from the sound of the Pentagon, Washington in general and especially Mr. Johnson, the fear-ridden hateful spites of J. Edgar Hoover, and the killing orders of anyone who wants to "boss" anything whether or not the work ought to be done.

It all comes down to the ring of bone. Where "ring" is what a bell does.

IV.

I once took a guided tour through a California winery and the guide, a young man about 20 years old, droned away with his memorized speech of facts and figures, chanting them perfectly in that guide-chant all of us have heard, and suddenly he stopped and yelled, "Whose kid is that!" A small child was determined to fall into a 500-gallon vat of wine.

The force of real speech slammed right against false speech was startling as a thunderclap, and not because he called out loudly.

I vowed never to release a poem of mine which couldn't at least equal the force of that guide's "Whose kid is that!" Pound said that poetry ought to be at least as well written as prose. I say that poetry ought to be at least as vigorous and useful as natural speech.

* * *

Tapes of readings are available through the Poetry Center, San Francisco State University, the University of California at Berkeley and Santa Barbara, and station KPFA in Berkeley. "A Round of English" is on a 33 rpm record produced by Mother, edited by Lewis MacAdams and Duncan McNaughton.

I shall always be grateful for the vigorous "underground" world of small presses and "little magazines," without which there would be no poetry in America.

[1968-1970]

Ed. Note: KPFA recordings of Lew Welch can be accessed at the Pacific Radio Archives— pacificaradioarchives.org

BOOK I

(1950 – 1960)

ON OUT

THIS BOOK IS FOR MAGDA

•

What strange pleasure do they get who'd

wipe whole worlds out,

ANYTHING,
to end our lives, our

wild idleness?

But we have charms against their rage—
must go on saying, "Look,
if nobody tried to live this way,
all the work of the world would be in vain."

And now and then a son, a daughter, hears it.

Now and then a son, a daughter

gets away

•

CHICAGO POEM

I lived here nearly 5 years before I could
    meet the middle western day with anything approaching
Dignity. It's a place that lets you
    understand why the Bible is the way it is:
Proud people cannot live here.

The land's too flat. Ugly sullen and big it
    pounds men down past humbleness. They
Stoop at 35 possibly cringing from the heavy and
    terrible sky. In country like this there
Can be no God but Jahweh.

In the mills and refineries of its south side Chicago
    passes its natural gas in flames
Bouncing like bunsens from stacks a hundred feet high.
    The stench stabs at your eyeballs.
The whole sky green and yellow backdrop for the skeleton
    steel of a bombed-out town.

Remember the movies in grammar school? The goggled men
    doing strong things in
Showers of steel-spark? The dark screen cracking light
    and the furnace door opening with a
Blast of orange like a sunset? Or an orange?

It was photographed by a fairy, thrilled as a girl, or
    a Nazi who wished there were people
Behind that door (hence the remote beauty), but Sievers,
    whose old man spent most of his life in there,
Remembers a "nigger in a red T-shirt pissing into the
    black sand."

It was 5 years until I could afford to recognize the ferocity.
    Friends helped me. Then I put some
Love into my house. Finally I found some quiet lakes
    and a farm where they let me shoot pheasant.

Standing in the boat one night I watched the lake go
     absolutely flat. Smaller than raindrops, and only
Here and there, the feeding rings of fish were visible a hundred
     yards away — and the Blue Gill caught that afternoon
Lifted from its northern lake like a tropical! Jewel at its ear
     Belly gold so bright you'd swear he had a
Light in there. His color faded with his life. A small
     green fish . . .

All things considered, it's a gentle and undemanding
     planet, even here. Far gentler
Here than any of a dozen other places. The trouble is
     always and only with what we build on top of it.

There's nobody else to blame. You can't fix it and you
     can't make it go away. It does no good appealing
To some ill-invented Thunderer
     Brooding above some unimaginable crag . . .

It's ours. Right down to the last small hinge it
     all depends for its existence
Only and utterly upon our sufferance.

Driving back I saw Chicago rising in its gases and I
     knew again that never will the
Man be made to stand against this pitiless, unparalleled
     monstrocity. It
Snuffles on the beach of its Great Lake like a
     blind, red, rhinoceros.
It's already running us down.

You can't fix it. You can't make it go away.
     I don't know what you're going to do about it,
But I know what I'm going to do about it. I'm just
     going to walk away from it. Maybe
A small part of it will die if I'm not around

     feeding it anymore.

A ROUND OF ENGLISH

for Philip Whalen

1.
The day I first woke up everybody had scabs on their eyes
    and I couldn't get to a mirror fast enough.

Everybody said that nothing had changed 'cause nothing ever could.

I thought I knew how to talk, but somebody showed up who
    could have heard it all, and I didn't have a thing to say.

Somebody else said, "Proust."

2.
It was all about a lady who gave vulgar soirees.
It was all about whales, and a harpoon sharp enough to shave with.
And "Look,
if you're really interested,
which I seriously begin to doubt,
you'll get it from the guys he stole it from."

She baréd her bosom
I whupped out m'knife
Carved my initials on her thin breast bone

"Thin brass dome, beautiful!
How'd you ever think of a thin brass dome?"

And somebody young as we were sagged into the room,
face all caked with blood and
clothes still damp with the natural leakage of a
5-day wine drunk:

"Well, I may be inverted,
but thank God I'm not insatiable."

There'll be BEANS BEANS BEANS enough for you and me
in the STORE
in the STORE

(Fry - HEIT)

3.

I always used a certain kind of notebook because it took the
    ink well.

"Saints are well fish"

Iridescent as horse fly
Ink should be
Should float upon the
Agéd scroll

And lost my rained-on *Swann's Way,* notes on the flyleaf,
"Water-lily Image," "His old Church." Lost
my footlocker full of notes
letters from cracking-up friends
hall notes from landlords
impassioned scribblings from urinal walls
carbons of letters (my own so young)

> *Please don't leave garbage in the*
> *hallway as garbage attracts termites*
> *and termites are the one thing we*
> *haven't had*

4.
After the Taozers and Hindoos and Parables of Zen,
the Writers by Century and all of their friends,
who knows how many sick Frenchmen and
all those 'Murcans comin' on free,
I never had time to read.

> *Came then to Chicago, to*
> *matriculate*
> *among the pros.*

•

I always expected to find, among those buttresses,
some rude Falstaffian man, surrounded by dogs,
polishing at the armour of his lord . . .
heard, instead, the voices of children, raised in song:

♪

Shakespeare Milton
Shakespeare Milton

Shelley as well
Shelley as well

Sarah something Teasdale
Sarah something Teasdale

Edith M. Bell
Edith M. Bell

5.
I wonder what I thought I'd find in all those books —
probably what's there from time to time, but
how could I have known that?

I wonder what it looked like then.

Some young horrifying thing all
muddy, and lurching, and
proud?

I sat brooding where the park is Japanese
with slanting rock and undernourished trees:

Is beauty that's blown from the oldest Sea
But beauty that's borne in the Mind's Eye? We
Who treasure it, just vain deluded men?

Pourquoi voulez-vous donc qu'il m'en souvienne

Taut hams
        shove her skirt
now to the right
        now to the left

There is nothing more to do today
nothing more to do

Nothing more to do today
nothing more to do

today
to do today

And no explanation but the oldest one of all:

> Lady, your visit alone is important to me
> though I'm often inadequate to your simple demand.
>
> For your sake I am unemployable in the world of Man,
> am often cruel to friends, and
> cannot keep my promises.
>
> Just when I think I know you, you take capricious form:
> chair to sea to rock to littlegirl reading on the
> supermarket steps; tongue between teeth, so
> serious!
> legs spread wide (a characteristic pose)
>
> O Waitress in a soiled uniform,
> finally bringing me my check

"And will that be all sir?"

>   Yes.

MEMO SATORI

There will be a policy meeting of key staff personnel in
Mr. Trout's office at 9 A.M., Monday. Please attend.

Well, here we go to bother out of all proportion:

      1) The scarcely bargain and a somewhat gain.
      2) The bought, unknown, incompetent.
      3) The might be someday done

$2^1/_2$ hours ago a bell rang

> *I live a winter morning,*
> *half-clothed in a dark room,*
> *trying to plan the day*

Drove through 16 miles of snow, slick roads, 35,000 speeding cars
& didn't kill a soul, or even
skid

> *The radiator lulls me now, my*
> *shoes begin to steam and dry*

              x   x   x   x   ✳

It happens, or can, almost anywhere, but here.
The sparrow at the Zoo:

        blurry little bird in his bath of dust
        just inside the camel's cage

dances off the pines and waves of a small Wisconsin Lake,
flickers on attention we can't quite hold still, till

      WHOP,   a

perfect clarity in
stopped time, and I

almost drove the boat against the swimmer's dock & drowned!

        never use a motor, man,

you gotta row
to go!

I FLY TO LOS ANGELES

Way down

In 1952 Chicago 10 above 0 in my gabardine raincoat handed
down to me by Dan Drew, too small, waiting in snow for a bus

I saw the silver glint of 4 motor airplane far up the sky, in the
clear cold and getting colder sun, the sunned-on snow drift
pink and floating violet against my tearing eyeballs and

Why? Why me way down here, all the rest flying, packed away
in too expensive airplanes, off, off to the whole world sliding
down mountains on little sticks, with bright-banded Norway
sweaters and 10 dollar sunglasses on?

Why me in Chicago Christmas Post Office 9.90 a day ain't got
no place to go in my gabardine coat?

So I caught pneumonia forgot to get my refund on the income
tax quit school got psychoanalyzed and

I've been buying warmer and warmer overcoats ever since.

I'm in those airplanes all the time now at Company Expense,
the finest in the air, free drinks pamperings airtravel cards and
right on schedule at the very best time of the day

While California my home sits quietly way on down there—
river stuffing his mud in the surf's mouth and a funny green
scum crawling between the folded mountains. I couldn't figure
it out, we'd had floods in California.

But I'm too crazy for this. It came too late or wrong or maybe
it costs too much that isn't money. Anyway people even the
squarest are starting to worry about me all the time and I get
more and more ashamed and tired.

I'm hiding in this airplane and they put me here for 2 days L.A. conference on Ivy Look, Chemise, and see the littlegirl night-gown looks Chemise? We'll take a little out of it and get the price down one full dime.

What happened among other things I bought *Gasoline* by Corso at the magazine stand (what a city!) of San Francisco airport

6 years after a vision of self-pity and a wrong vow reading the beautiful poems of Gregory Corso at Company Expense and weeping when he said Hello

Wept I don't deny it when the beautiful little wop-hood said Hello and the whole unwrittenness I am came boiling out my carcass thinking He's beautiful beautiful that boy

And how did he come by it?

Beside the point (you can read his poems in his book bought mine for mine) so finally I had this vision of how the waste and where the words and visions and what else got despite the many many good things—driveling away up 14,000 feet

But very discreetly alone in a window seat way up front against the partition at Company Expense in my new best gray business suit flying over all that cloud-banked sea coast

Till Stewardess (and me way up there on the high glint silver thing that ground me, almost, all the way—out, out at last on that big bird) said

"Don't you want to freshen up sir" handing me a rag with wet sweet scents on it and I reached out and took it eagerly and knew all at once she thought

Drunk or sick (as well she must) and me? Me the only one-on this old plane? Most likely so

But O that rag felt fine! I missed it when I grabbed and caught the tray napkin too, Stewardess said "just the yellow one sir, not the blue" very helpfully—like I say the squarest start to dig, what difference if only in the dimmest way

Out. Way outside. As anybody else could see 6 years ago or
12 and I've known every third 5 minutes all along.

Thank you Corso! Thank you all the patient people! Mary most
of all and Whalen and Snyder and Kepecs and Williams and
Wilson and all who loved me once and got too busy and I've
been, even, very patient too

But I can't do it anymore. I can't get myself so close against
them they won't see me anymore (my sinecure at 31 with 7600
a year and me with everything left over and not a minute's time
to do it with)

Outside and noticed and grounded and dumb and

Thank you even Stewardess when she caught me later with the
puke bag "Oh no! You don't need that?" and I said

No I just wondered about this curious message:

FOR MOTION SICKNESS

ONLY. PLEASE, NO REFUSE!

And I won't! I can't anymore. How can I refuse God Damn
it 31 years old outside and noticed and much too tired and

flying

1. AFTER ANACREON

When I drive cab
  I am moved by strange whistles and wear a hat.

When I drive cab
  I am the hunter. My prey leaps out from where it hid,
  beguiling me with gestures.

When I drive cab
  all may command me, yet I am in command of all who do.

When I drive cab
  I am guided by voices descending from the naked air.

When I drive cab
  A revelation of movement comes to me. They wake now.
  Now they want to work or look around. Now they want
  drunkenness and heavy food. Now they contrive to love.

When I drive cab
  I bring the sailor home from the sea. In the back of
  my car he fingers the pelt of his maiden.

When I drive cab
  I watch for stragglers in the urban order of things.

When I drive cab
  I end the only lit and waitful thing in miles of
  darkened houses.

2. PASSENGER POEM, THE NURSE

I don't like cats kittens are all right I guess
you can love 'em when they're little, like people,
but then they grow up and take advantage of you

and how can you love 'em anymore?

3. PASSENGER POEM, MRS. ANGUS

There's lots of death down there
and a fish the Spanish people eat
couldn't get me near one
red they are, like meat
Bonita.

A famous jockey and two other lads,
and him with a big race comin' up Sunday,
went out at night in a little boat
and they was washed I think
to a place of reptiles, and eaten, for
none of 'em was ever found.

Yon place scares me.

4. PASSENGER POEM, THE MAILMAN

"I understand you had a parade today," I said,
flipping the meter over and driving into traffic.
Without so much as a yes he got right into it
(carefully, with many pauses):

> *We wore*
> *regulation letter-carrier's*
> *uniforms,*
> *except for the leggin's*
> *of course, and the*
> *helmets. Whatdayacallem?*

"You mean the kind of hat Teddy Roosevelt wore when
he went to Africa to shoot lions, Pith Helmets?"

> *That's right*
> *helmets.*
>
> *Fellow next to me carried*
> *the association banner.*
>
> *I carried*
> *the American Flag.*
>
> *It looked real*
> *nice.*

5. TOP OF THE MARK

for John Wieners

I guess it's only natural that they
go about their planet as they do
all night long:

> Top of the Mark, St. Francis,
> Fairmont, Sir Francis Drake

What a price they pay for what they see!

> *I cannot help them*
> *I will not cheat them*

Yesterday I drove the actual Cab of Heaven   .   I am
     Leo   .   I was born this way

     my mane is longer than the sun

BARBARA/VAN GOGH POEM

Barbara, think what'd happen if Van Gogh'd ever seen
    eucalyptus trees
Or knew my coves on up this coast where nobody ever goes
    firewood everywhere   .   steep rock   .   birds

I give you my city of daemonic friends and sweet-smoke
    saintly rooms where I could love you 5 slow ways
You who dream my suicide and claim to want beginning

I sold my wedding ring and bought cheap gold for your ears
    where the moon is even wilder than you think   .
    there is just one cricket   .   and the light we would
    lay by, shattered

More than in that Dutchman's funny eye

LEO, PLEASED

What Chaucer used to call "Love Longynge" is only
hunger
Only drives the mind to fancy feasts
when all we need is this
fed feeling

You,
Who crouch to my Lion,
Cuff me and play, thy
Notch flowing Rum and Honey . . .

*—honey and essences of rum
rum and the essence of almonds—*

How can we tell them strong enough dangerous
Nations of us taught to
Starve till we almost learn to live that way
Tremble & twitch through dark unnecessary dreams fingers
Numb
Whole bodies shy, suspicious
Bodies but
(not so secretly) powered to

Now let's have chunks of citrus in a wooden bowl!
Now let's have eggs poached in milk & paprika!

—sweeten my coffee with honey
0 sweeten my coffee with rum—

•

Lion

Lying on his side

"golden syrup"

(within the belly, bees begin to build)

LEO, IN ABSENCE OF FIRE

Tonight the fires are all outside,
I cannot manage them

matches will not strike
are never in the pockets I reach for

no smoldering of incense
(though I thought a flame leaped up)

and a moth got stuck in the
wax of my candle . . .

I, Leo
Leo my sign and Star
Leo my Star as the World has a Star

(the feather shaggy: a flame)

O Lady why did you not come?
Lady.   Anne.

O Anne I taste your skin
        all last week you lay in the sun & got so brown

Your skin so salt . . .

        no white gas for the Coleman
        wood in the woodstove just won't burn

        moth

        smashed in the wax of my candle

Commentary by the Red Monk

*Anyone who confuses his mistress with his muse
is asking for real trouble from both of them.*

SONG OF A SELF

If this is what life is,
Could one of your Gods do it better?

I make what I see, and I make what I hear
with Eye and my animal eye—
with ear and my Auditing Ear . . .

> *full*
> *full of my gift*
> *I am never*
> *left out and afraid*

And this what the song is
(all of you waking and working and going to bed)

I sing what you'd know if you took time to hear,
I know what you'd learn if you had cause to care
Envy my wildness if you will . . .

> *full*
> *full of my gift*
> *I am often*
> *left out and afraid*

And this all my art is
(that stays at the distance the stage is)

You turn from my songs into one another's arms,
As I, who have taken you all to my heart,
Would sometime be taken to heart . . .

> *full*
> *full of my gift*
> *I am only*
> *left out and afraid*

Commentary by the Red Monk

*Except for things like the Yaws, there is no suffering
unless we invent someone to suffer the suffering.*

ENTIRE SERMON BY THE RED MONK

1.
We invent ourselves.
2.
We invent ourselves out of ingredients we didn't
choose, by a process we can't control.
3.
The Female Impersonator, and the Sadistic Marine can
each trace himself *back* to the same stern, or weak, father.
4.
Usually it's less dramatic. He was only indifferently
a basketball player. Now he is selling cars.
5.
The baby on the floor cannot be traced, *forward,*
to anything.
6.
It's all your own fault then.
7.
On all kinds of baby purpose, you invented whoever
you think you are. Out of ingredients you couldn't
choose, by a process you can't control.

All you really say is, "Love me for myself alone."
8.
It is also possible to *uninvent* yourself. By a process
you can't control.
9.
But you invented Leo.   Forget it.

IN SAFEWAY PARKING LOTS, OLD MEN DRIVE SLOWLY. BACKWARDS.

Leo, with his cock of Port,
70 miles-an-hour,
passing trains:

The last time I was in Amarillo,
I smoked my first cigar,
and Roosevelt died.

THE FIRST WARM DAY OF THE YEAR

Hundreds of us,
haunch to haunch on
        every bench in
Central Park

eyes closed, faces pointing
        at the Sun, we're

turning

as the Sun turns

APOTHEOSIS OF LEO

Digesting a succulent Gazelle,
"Yum Yum," said Leo
and turned into a giant round rock.

The rock said,

"It's cold out here. I think I'll
spin around that Star

for a couple of Kalpas."

And Leo laughed, for he was the Sun,

and said,

"Yum Yum"

CIRCLE POEMS

Whenever I have a day off, I write a new poem.
Does this mean you shouldn't work, or that you
write best on your day off?

For example, this is the poem I wrote today.

When he was 20, he understood some of the secrets of
life, and undertook to write them down so simply that
even an idiot could understand.
"For," he reasoned, "if I can't do that, I don't
understand it myself."

He proved himself right.
When he was 50, he didn't understand it himself.

"Why is it," he said, "that no matter what you say, a woman always takes it personally?"

"I never do," she said.

John said, "Then I met that short fat guy with the neat little beard, with a name like dawn."

"You mean George Abend?"

"Yeah."

"Abend means evening."

SEASONS

Spring

do with hills
with a pale branch do

do with hills and
do with every dale

for every single pale pale
tulip
a rhododendron
done

wrench a branch do
do wrench a branch do

do

        •

Summer

nine golden mistresses
one weaving bees in her hair

with silk
and with the wings thereof
she fashioned 20 bunches

then she had a perfect ring

a star

Fall

Wet
the dead leaves stick upon the hillside

among them
                beads of a light rain
gathered in her short-cropped hair
                                the lean girl walks

tweeds

befitting her.

Break not upon a 4-foot hedge the
crisp leaf dangling

shallowly the river flows

Winter

Alice Herlihy had hard hands
had hands made hard by
working for her father with stones

it seemed as though the
stones would grow from the land
in wintertime
to be gathered as a crop and
stacked into neat low walls
lacing the land
separating flocks

Alice used to also sit and sew
sitting in a little wooden rocking chair

which creaked.

ELIOTICA REVISITED

> Patina accumulates
> permits fruition
>
> the stair creaks
> as we ascend

To tell you this did I assume the salient cat
Whispering of Sweeney, the knot in a cravat
And "Do, Mrs. Proctor, do tell again of
Escapades by shores of Zuyder Zee"

To tell you this did I remain transitional.
Certainly never here
Partaking of that other, animal, grace
Nor there,
In death's green kingdom.

And do not send felicitations due an earned repose
My one remembrance of
An untransmuted Love
I labelled "cogitations"

Because I told you only this
Because I could tell you only this
Not here the stair
Not even the stair
Creaking, as we ascend

Yet I have known the burdened branch
Bird song, and, quietly
The branch

And thought I saw my corpse rolled twice
In the brown course of the river
And thought I saw one rise
Did you see one rise? Standing
Above new legs, peeping
About, finding so absurdly grave
That sudden nakedness—

Such moments flit with sound of ringing commonplace
Obsequious helloes to greet
My smooth, remembered, face.

SKUNK CABBAGE

1
Slowly in the swamps unfold
great yellow petals of a
savage thing, a
tropic thing—

While no stilt-legged birds watch,
no monkey screams,
those great yellow petals
unfold.

2
Rank plant.

CORINNA'S GONE A-PREYING

Corinna's gone a-preying
she might not know

but see her tilt her head
listening as a robin to a rustle in the grass &

see her hold her breasts so high
see the way she feels her thigh
tautly slide beneath her skirt

    take her now
    take her now

she doesn't even know

Corinna's gone a-preying

ATLANTIS WAS CRETE

a poem for magick-dabblers

A long time ago, on a clear day,
hairy little men with greedy eyes sat
looking across blue water   fingering
sharp bronze & breathing quick:

>"Sissy Island!
>Bull Jumpers!
>Their females lift their breasts in
>   cages of silver . . .
>One took feathers & wax and stuck them into
>wings & his boy fell all the down from
>Sun (like anybody could have said he would)"

So they sacked it.
Burned it down to
Myth and sheep farms ever since

Dreamed Atlantis in our later brains

You can walk about that palace now
flush, I suppose, those oldest toilets in the world &
eat a dish of fish-head soup with
natives looted 35 hundred years ago

who do not know or
give a damn about it

A PARABLE OF WASPS

They went, like wasps,
down to the riverside,

gathered up the silt in balls &
brought it here for building.

Cell heaped up on cell, their
juices turning silt to stone

       —frantic creatures
        sealing themselves

in stone
a humming stone

pelted by wasps

hail stones whacking
a boulder

YOU CAN'T BURLESQUE IT ANYMORE, – 1956

The headline said:

> Nixon Stoned in Peru

Eisenhower said:

> This is a time for greatness

And the Daughters of the Eastern Star had a slogan:

> Walk with your face toward the sun
> Let the shadows fall behind

A St. Louis car dealer said:

> Nothin' about this recession couldn't be cured
> By the sale of 2 million automobiles

A sign in Chicago buses said:

> Every day 11,000 babies are born in America.
> This means
> New business
> New jobs
> New opportunities

A poster on the mail trucks said:

> Be fully informed, read a magazine.

They cancelled our postage stamps with:

> Pray for Peace

And Birdy Tebbitts, manager of the Cincinnati Redlegs, said:

> Fear of a bat
> Fear of getting spiked
> Fear of the crowd
> I don't care who they are
> All ballplayers
> Are afraid.

IN ANSWER TO A QUESTION FROM P. W.

In Mexico I'll finish the novel I'll write, rough, while
     fire-watching in Oregon.
The problem is, what kind of typewriter to pack in?

I ought to be able to live 6 months in Mexico on what I
     earn on the Mountain in 4.
They say you can buy dirty books down there.

Since they give you horses to pack things in, how would it
     be if I took in a big old typewriter and left it there?
They don't give you horses to pack things out.

Going to Mexico by motorcycle would be the coolest, but
     Thoreau warns against any undertaking that
     requires new clothes.
Walking is pure, but I haven't achieved simplicity yet.
I'll never willingly hitchhike again.

Next winter I can buy Snyder's Austin for $200, but how
     can I get the money together?
They repossessed my Oldsmobile.
I've never made the foreign-country scene.

Like the sign over the urinal: "You hold your future
     in your hand."
Or what the giant black whore once said, in the back of my cab:

        "Man, you sure do love diggin' at my
        titties, now stop that. We get where
        we going you can milk me like a
        Holstein, but I gotta see your
        money first."

COMPLEYNT AT 38

All of us having love problems
"the stars are bad right now"
Everybody breaking up and regrouping
            cautious. clumsy.

Too late, now, to run about with blossoms in our teeth
or bleakly moan on a lady's porch

"Unconvincing"

            our publishers like to say

Already not so young anymore
what is this we guard?

VIRGIN AT THE BUS STOP

            Think of the flat little
            unsucked nipples on her
            big new breasts!

            Come,
            Let's make a meal for some lucky

            Bastard!

CONCERNING THE MURDER OF BIRDS

I wonder what happened to Dickey Schade.

Dickey Schade was bald at 22. He had a secondary
male characteristic.

Then he got nervous and they wired up his brain and
threw the switch.

I can't think why.

What would Tom Edison say? Tom Payne? à Becket?
Tom Tit?

"Here there is no stone on which two birds might
meet," said Dickey Schade.

I heard the snap of hymens!
I heard the gurgle of virginal blood! Clubbed
children in the street, the
shriek of an angry
Drab!

How about *that* Tom Tit !

"Marshall Kolin is a
slimy bear!" said

Dickey Schade.

GOLDILOCKS

for Robin Blaser

Somewhere in my head:
Robert Southey. Three Bears. Porridge &
bad beds
incompetent Laureate finally lucking out a story

but Southey!!?

so I phoned you, Robin, knowing you're captive in a Library—
"Yes. You're right.
Southey. *The Doctor*

Dr. Dove and Mr. Williams."

. . . a mannerless old woman, changed, by Scudder, 1881,
to "Silver Hair," it then became Goldilocks . . .

changed by
mouths of
Uncles, Fathers, Mothers

Goldilocks !   Goldilocks !

O

Yes!   She

does know how to make us call

her name

27 November 1964

THE FOUR STORIES OF APPLE

(Sermon by the Red Monk)

"Appletreeforyouandme AppleApple
Appletreeforyouandme Apple
Apple,"

> I was singing,
> at Sonny Rollins,
> heard, then

four great stories of apple:

1.   (The Wisest Man who ever lived)

"It took me 9 days to realize I was once perfectly
happy. I was eating an apple."

2.   (A very smart man)

"That hurt. I'm sure glad this tree isn't taller."
"*Taller!?*"

3.   (A very good man)

Half starved on a high trail, his bag full of seeds:

"The people are kind of backwards in Oklahoma."

4.   (Beyond guessing)

Put an apple inside your head.
Shoot at it.

(Do not use a mirror, a gun, a bow & arrow, or anything else.)

HIKING POEM / HIGH SIERRA

Measurements can never tell it:

    4,000 feet down into a canyon and
    4,500 feet up the other side,
    in a little under 8 miles, with a
    30 pound pack on my back . . . or

Several times up and down the stairs of the
Empire State Building, in
one afternoon, with
30 pound pack on my back

        BEAT BARD
        BEATS BUILDING
       "Pooped," says Poet

How many million years to miracle human shape now
working,

    "As no other animal"

just to look around

1.
Ant Lion traps in the trail dust.

    —thumbs under pack straps
    I can only look down

thousands upon thousands of them!
perfect cones (quivering at the bottom)

Are Ant Lion traps worse than how we dammed Hetch Hetchy?

"forgive SF housewives
all their washing"

Scarring it, all of us, in our fashion.

Grouse,
huge clumsy birds,
crash around in the pine trees

breaking branches

2.
Absolute fatigue perhaps way to Perfect Total Enlightenment?

my last poor shred of sense decides to count my steps

900   901   902   903   904   905

"surely half a mile" becomes, thereby,
a little less than 300 yards

THE MIRACLE OF THE HUMAN MIND!

12 hours going in, counting and cursing all the way,
6 hours coming out, free.

*Trails go nowhere.
They end exactly
where you stop.*

3.
Mile-high humps of granite are like bubbles in our
Cream-of-Wheat

hundred-foot trees like tiny moss on mile-high
               humps of Cream-of-Wheat
Inverted Ant Lion traps, quivering?
On top?

An interesting play of the mind, but only
an interesting play of the mind:
The scales are off my eyes . . .

I saw humanity merge into one last giant
junky, waiting (for The Man), on some last
barren ridge, last,
most horrible vision of Man-Hooked Man . . .

Or make it gentler. Nail a sign to one of these trees.

                VOTE HERE

for example

4.
after dinner I took a walk
and She said so sweetly
(finally finding me alone)

          Why do men look for lost cities
          when lost groves grow
          just over the next knoll and the
          next, and next . . .

And all that has always sickened me,
all I know my kind will always be,
dropped away again
into the same old poem

          you bear with me.

FOUR STUDIES IN PERCEPTION

1. *Laurels*

A grove of Laurel grows in the city park.
It grows whether I look at it or not.

It grows whether I look at it or not,
by a path deliberately unintended (unattended).

I can find it.   I can see it.   I can sing:

> *Magical Tree!*
> *Leaf in my Mother's stew!*
> *Crown!   Chew*
> *thy leaves to brighten*
> *color in my eyes?*

But all of it,
Singer, Song, the Grove itself,
disappears, instantly,
if I only look another way.

If I only look another way, I make
Bulldozers, Baseball Players, and, later
Owls

To become enamoured of our Powers is to lose them, at once!

It grows whether I look at it or not.
If, as I plan, I wish to chew these leaves and
braid myself a wreath,
I cannot wish the Grove to grow on Taraval Street

And all our Certainties are
tinier thoughts, even,

than that.

2. Fern Trees

Near the grove of Laurel is a stand of Giant Fern Trees.
I can find it.   I can see it.   I can sing:

> *Hey Old Feather Tree!*   *0 Strange!*
> *Big Bush!*
> *Ancient!*   *Unchanged!*

How do I see "ancientness," "unchanged," all
sharks, lizards, cockroach . . .

> *plaster reconstruction of a pre-historic*
> *forest in Chicago museum strange bugs*
> *sitting on the fronds Nevada fossils in a*
> *sandy rock my preference for cave-like*
> *rooms recurrent dreams of giant lizards*
> *waking mis-takes on beaches sandy deserts*
> *rock-mass or driftwood seen as giant lizard*
> *darting at me, terrible sight on trail*
> *Chameleon in the jaws of Snake changing*
> *color changing color changing color in the*
> *different teeth of death, and I pitied*
> *Snake his awful meal . . .*

is "Ancientness":

A Pre-Historic Giant Fern Forest now

GROWING!

(before my very eyes)

3. *Brown Small Bird*

The Nightingale will always be a mythical bird.
Did you ever see one outside Poetry?
The Nightingale is named into anonymity, like a Monk,
like the celebrated girl who is only beautiful.

What a different thing it was when
Wild-Bird took
actual berries from my hand.

Blessed, I wanted statues made of it, a
city named, or something

Brown, small, bird.
Not to be known by his name anymore

than you, or me

4. *Re-echo*

The mind wants all our mountains wadded into one.
Frightened, on the mountain, the mind
looks back at itself:

> *"I climbed Hood once."*
> *"McKinley's twice as high."*

Remember our honeymoon in Switzerland?

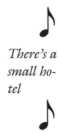

*There's a
small ho-
tel*

"Listen, I
ast for that song because I
like that song. You guys mess around with it I
can't even hear the tune."

> If the tune's so important, man,
> why don't you go into the can and
> whistle it to yourself?

WOBBLY ROCK

for Gary Snyder

"I think I'll be the Buddha of this place"

and sat himself
down

    1.
It's a real rock

    (believe this first)

Resting on actual sand at the surf's edge:
Muir Beach, California

    (like everything else I have
    somebody showed it to me and I found it by myself)

Hard common stone
Size of the largest haystack
It moves when hit by waves
Actually shudders

    (even a good gust of wind will do it
    if you sit real still and keep your mouth shut)

Notched to certain center it
Yields and then comes back to it:

Wobbly tons

2.

Sitting here you look below to other rocks
Precisely placed as rocks of Ryoanji:
Foam like swept stones

    (the mind getting it all confused again:
    "snow like frosting on a cake"
    "rose so beautiful it don't look real")

Isn't there a clear example here
Stone garden shown to me by
Berkeley painter I never met
A thousand books and somebody else's boatride ROCKS

    (garden)

EYE

    (nearly empty despite this clutter-image all
    the opposites cancelling out a
    CIRCULAR process: *Frosting-snow)*

Or think of the monks who made it 4 hundred 50 years ago
Lugged the boulders from the sea
Swept to foam original gravelstone from sea

    (first saw it, even then, when finally they
    all looked up the
    instant AFTER it was made)

And now all rocks are different and
All the spaces in between

    (which includes about everything)

The instant
After it is made

3.
I have been in many shapes before I attained congenial form
All those years on the beach, lifetimes . . .

When I was a boy I used to watch the Pelican:
It always seemed his wings broke
And he dropped, like scissors, in the sea . . .
Night fire flicking the shale cliff
Balls tight as a cat after the cold swim
Her young snatch sandy . . .

> *I have travelled*
> *I have made a circuit*
> *I have lived in 14 cities*
> *I have been a word in a book*
> *I have been a book originally*

Dychymig Dychymig: (riddle me a riddle)

> Waves and the sea. If you
> take away the sea

Tell me what it is

4.

Yesterday the weather was nice there were lots of people
Today it rains, the only other figure is far up the beach

(by the curve of his body I know he leans against
the tug of his fishingline: there is no separation)

Yesterday they gathered and broke gathered and broke like
Feeding swallows dipped down to pick up something ran back to
Show it
And a young girl with jeans rolled to mid-thigh ran
Splashing in the rain creek

*"They're all so damned happy—
why can't they admit it?"*

Easy enough until a little rain shuts beaches down . . .

Did it mean nothing to you Animal that turns this
Planet to a smoky rock?
Back among your quarrels
How can I remind you of your gentleness?

Jeans are washed
Shells all lost or broken
Driftwood sits in shadow boxes on a tracthouse wall

Like swallows you were, gathering
Like people I wish for . . .

cannot even tell this to that fisherman

5.

3 of us in a boat the size of a bathtub   .   pitching in
slow waves   .   fish poles over the side   .   oars

We rounded a point of rock and entered a small cove

Below us:
            fronds of kelp
            fish
            crustaceans
            eels
Then us
            then rocks at the cliff's base
            starfish
            (hundreds of them sunning themselves)
            final starfish on the highest rock then
Cliff
            4 feet up the cliff a flower
            grass
            further up more grass
            grass over the cliff's edge
            branch of pine then
Far up the sky

            a hawk

Clutching to our chip we are jittering in a spectrum
Hung in the film of this narrow band
Green
            to our eyes only

6.

On a trail not far from here
Walking in meditation
We entered a dark grove
And I lost all separation in step with the
Eucalyptus as the trail walked back beneath me

Does it need to be that dark or is
Darkness only its occasion
Finding it by ourselves knowing
Of course
Somebody else was there before . . .

I like playing that game
Standing on a high rock looking way out over it all:

"I think I'll call it the Pacific"

Wind water
Wave rock
Sea sand

    (there is no separation)

Wind that wets my lips is salt
Sea breaking within me balanced as the
Sea that floods these rocks. Rock
Returning to the sea, easily, as
Sea once rose from it. It
Is a sea rock

    (easily)

I am
Rocked by the sea

TWO LIKE VILLANELLES

They're tearing down all the Victorian Mansions and
building Freeways in Portland Oregon & everywhere

               "and the rough places
               shall be plane"

In a landscape of ruined buildings,
on a small rock wheeling about the heavens and
      comin' on green to crack sidewalks,
you looked so beautiful picking blackberries
      all the long summer afternoon.

The berries!
Berries made fountains of fruit and thorn on
      rubble, iron fence and gate, on
basement steps to basement now just
berry-pit.

And you!
You looked so beautiful picking blackberries,
      long black hair in the summer sun, black eyes
glancing up to where I stood

In a landscape of ruined buildings,
on a small green rock

      wheeling about the heavens

For all the Wet Green Girls

I found myself, green girls, in a month like May,
in a green green garden at the break of day

all around me gray rain beat
and the cage that I am was an empty zoo

in a garden, girls, at a break like May
in the first wet light of the sun

when, from a rock in the arbor leapt
a sleeping cat, through

gray green cages of deserted zoo
where I found myself on a breaking day

as bright rain beat upon the garden stone
where the lept cat left his belly print

alone, young girls, when my head unbent
in a green green garden at the break of day

and I saw what came
and I watched what went

Green Girls

LINES TO AN URBAN DAWN

the rising sun
pries the pigeon from beneath his wing
wakes in a doorway the old man
who slept in his coat last night, and

makes the water seem more cold
spilling from a shallow bowl
held high by four greek hands.

    —there they meet
    timing it perfectly

pigeon setting wings and
pushing from the roof's edge
just as the man got up.

man and pigeon bathe in the fountain
part
pasture on the city and
will meet again in public parks.

NOTES FROM A PIONEER ON A SPECK IN SPACE

Few things that grow here poison us.
Most of the animals are small.
Those big enough to kill us do it in a way
Easy to understand, easy to defend against.
The air, here, is just what the blood needs.
We don't use helmets or special suits.

The Star, here, doesn't burn you if you
Stay outside as much as you should.
The worst of our winters is bearable.
Water, both salt and sweet, is everywhere.
The things that live in it are easily gathered.
Mostly, you can eat them raw with safety and pleasure.

Yesterday my wife and I brought back
Shells, driftwood, stones, and other curiosities
Found on the beach of the immense
Fresh-water Sea we live by.
She was all excited by a slender white stone which:
"Exactly fits the hand!"

I couldn't share her wonder;
Here, almost everything does.

[I RATE MY FURY WITH THE]

I rate my fury with the
bumblebee, banging at my windowpane,

though I open it, I
always have to shoo him on his way

and the next day (believing it
really worked) the same thing furiously:

missing it, an
eighth of an inch away

not necessarily straight ahead,
you understand, and

just as seldom
up

BOOK II

(1960 – 1964)

HERMIT POEMS

For Lloyd Reynolds

PREFACE TO HERMIT POEMS, THE BATH

At last it is raining, the first sign of spring.
The Blue Jay gets all wet.

Frost-flowers, tiny bright and dry like
inch high crystal trees or sparkling silver mold,
acres of them, on heaps of placer boulders all around me,
are finally washing away. They were beautiful.
And the big trees rising, dark, behind them.

This canyon is so steep we didn't get sun since late November,
my "CC" shack and I. Obsolete. The two of us.
He for his de-funct agency.
I for this useless Art?

> *"Oughtta come by more often, Lewie,
> you get shack simple."*

big winter boom of the river
crunch of boots on the icy trail to it

kerosene lantern even in the daytime   golden light

inside

I think I'll bathe in
Spring-rain tin-roof clatter of it
all begins to melt away.
The bath a ritual here, the way it used to be.

> *Vat & Cauldron*
> *Kettle Pot & Tub*
> *Stoke the Stove till Cherry*

Naked, he clambers over boulders to his spring.
He dips two buckets full and scampers back.
Filling the many vessels on his stove, he starts
to rave.

I hear Incantations!
I hear voices of the Wise Old Men and
songs of the Addled Girls!

Moss! Astonishing green!
All that time the rocks were, even.

Hopping on it, wet, that Crested Blue!

Robin bedraggled.   Warm rain finally.   Spring.

[NOT YET 40, MY BEARD IS ALREADY WHITE.]

Not yet 40, my beard is already white.
Not yet awake, my eyes are puffy and red,
        like a child who has cried too much.

What is more disagreeable
than last night's wine?

I'll shave.
I'll stick my head in the cold spring and
look around at the pebbles.
Maybe I can eat a can of peaches.

Then I can finish the rest of the wine,
write poems till I'm drunk again,
and when the afternoon breeze comes up

I'll sleep until I see the moon
and the dark trees
and the nibbling deer

and hear
the quarreling coons

[I KNOW A MAN'S SUPPOSED TO HAVE HIS HAIR CUT SHORT,]

I know a man's supposed to have his hair cut short,
but I have beautiful hair.
like to let it grow into a long bronze mane.

In my boots. In my blue wool shirt.
With my rifle slung over my shoulder
among huge boulders in the dark ravine,

I'm the ghost roan stallion.
Leif Ericson.
The beautiful Golden Girl!

In summer I usually cut it all off.
I do it myself, with scissors and a
little Jim Beam.

How disappointed everybody is.

Months and months go by before they can
worry about my hairdo

and the breeze
is so cool

[APPARENTLY WASPS]

Apparently wasps
work all their only summer at the nest,
so that new wasps work
all their only summer at the nest,
et cetera.

All my lizards lost their tails, mating.
Six green snakes ate all my frogs.
Butterflies do very odd things with their tongues.

There seems to be no escaping it.
I planted nine tomato plants and water them.
I replaced my rotten stoop with a
clean Fir block.

Twelve new poems in less than a week!

[I BURN UP THE DEER IN MY BODY.]

I burn up the deer in my body.
I burn up the tree in my stove.

I seldom let a carrot go to seed, and I
grind up every kind of grain.

How can I be and never be an
inconvenience to others, here,

where only the Vulture is absolutely pure

and in the Chicago River
are carp?

Step out onto the Planet.
Draw a circle a hundred feet round.

Inside the circle are
300 things nobody understands, and, maybe
nobody's ever really seen.

How many can you find?

[THE EMPRESS HERSELF SERVED TEA TO SU TUNG-PO,]

The Empress herself served tea to Su Tung-po,
and ordered him escorted home by
Ladies of the Palace, with torches.

I forgot my flashlight.
Drunk, I'll never get across this
rickety bridge.

Even the Lady in the Sky abandons me.

[WHENEVER I MAKE A NEW POEM,]

Whenever I make a new poem,
the old ones sound like gibberish.
How can they ever make sense in a book?

Let them say:
"He seems to have lived in the mountains.
He traveled now and then.
When he appeared in cities,
he was almost always drunk.

"Most of his poems are lost.
Many of those we have were found in
letters to his friends.

"He had a very large number of friends."

[THE IMAGE, AS IN A HEXAGRAM:]

The image, as in a Hexagram:

The hermit locks his door against the blizzard.
He keeps the cabin warm.

All winter long he sorts out all he has.
What was well started shall be finished.
What was not, should be thrown away.

In spring he emerges with one garment
and a single book.

The cabin is very clean.

Except for that, you'd never guess
anyone lived there.

[I SAW MYSELF]

I saw myself
a ring of bone
in the clear stream
of all of it

and vowed,
always to be open to it
that all of it
might flow through

and then heard
"ring of bone" where
ring is what a

bell does

BOOK III

(1960 – 1964)

THE WAY BACK

THE WAY BACK

HE PREPARES TO TAKE LEAVE OF HIS HUT

And They, The Blessed Ones, said to him,
"Beautiful trip, Avalokiteshvara.
You never have to go back there again."

And he said, "Thank you very much, but I think I will.
Those people need all the help they can get."

      Not that I'm on the
      Other Side of the River, you understand,
      except literally.

      To get to the shack I found, you have to
      cross a rickety bridge of splintered boards, of
      cables, rusty, small, not really
      tied anymore to Alder trees.

      And a Raccoon takes a shit on it,
      almost every day, right where I have to
      step to get across.

      And should I wonder if it's
      fear, malevolence, or chance that
      makes him do this thing to me,

      when nothing's really stained by it,
      and yesterday a Butterfly sat down on it

           Butterfly on a Coon Turd
           A wet, blue, Jay

And even that is just a
pretty imitation of a
state of Mind I don't possess

or even seek, right now, or
wait for anymore.

"Why should it be so hard to give up
seeking something you know you can't possess?"

"Who ever said it was easy?"

HE ASKS FOR GUIDANCE

Avalokiteshvara, Buddha of Compassion, Original
Bodhisattva, Who spoke the Prajnaparamita Sutra
of the heart,

Kannon in Japan, Kuan-Yin in China, Chenrezig in
Tibet, No God, but guide, O
Countless thousands of returning men and women
of every place and time,

as Virgil for Dante, through Dante's Hell,

please guide me through Samsara.

HE WRITES TO THE DONOR OF HIS BOWL

November 25, 1962

Albert,

The last thing I ate in the beautiful bowl you made & gave me
was a Salmon Chippino (perhaps misspelled & not in my
Webster's dictionary)

Old Bill Allen & I went out for mushrooms, but it's been too long
since rain & the mushrooms are wormy or rotten or both

& while I went to the car for a pull on the wine-jug Bill got all
excited pointing at the creek & motioning me downstream
("you pitch, I'll catch" I always say to the old men on this river
who can't very well scramble across wet rocks anymore, though
they shoot very straight)

& he shot this salmon with his 30-30 & I got wet to the knees
catching it as it washed downstream (not being able to pick
my spot)

What he didn't know is, salmon stay nicely in that pool so there
isn't any hurry, but he hurried, & I barely got the cap back on
the bottle & splashed in the creek & grabbed it (both hands just
above the tail & lift — that way they seem unable to move, as I
learned on commercial fishing boats)

You boil potatoes, celery, onions & garlic in a little water & when
they are almost done you dump in chunks of Salmon (or whatever
fish or crabs) A little later add a can of stewed tomatoes.

It was good fish stew made better by the bowl you made.

Thank you,

HE THANKS HIS WOODPILE

The wood of the madrone burns with a flame at once
lavender and mossy green, a color you sometimes see in a sari.

Oak burns with a peppery smell.

For a really hot fire, use bark.
You can crack your stove with bark.

All winter long I make wood stews:

Poem to stove to woodpile to stove to
typewriter.   woodpile.   stove.

and can't stop peeking at it!
can't stop opening up the door!
can't stop giggling at it

"Shack Simple"

crazy as Han Shan as
Wittgenstein in his German hut, as
all the others ever were and are

       Ancient Order of the Fire Gigglers

who walked away from it, finally,
kicked the habit, finally, of Self, of
man-hooked Man

      (which is not, at last, estrangement)

A SONG TO HIS SECRET FARM

for Robert Creeley

Grow, little plant!
Show those who waste my time and thee
How good it is to be
As any weed.

       —Jungle Thing!

Fear not though deer shall
Surely clip thy life, be
Stoical,
Like I

It was for Love you came so far
To germinate

And die!

FAREWELL TO HIS BIRDS AND ANIMALS

Richer than the richest Falconer,
I hold my hawks and canyons light as time.

"Just happening along," as they say

        for a flutter
        for a wing-fold terrifying
        drop

(a small explosion on the ground!)

        dust & feathers
        rodent squeek

(his dinner's dangling down!)

HE PRAISES HIS CANYONS & PEAKS

Driving out to Callahan, you get the setting for it all:

      Cloud-shrouded gorges!
      Foggy trees!

      I can't see the ridges anymore!
      River?

Big Sung landscape scroll a

mile high and

      longer than I'll ever know!

HE GREETS, AGAIN, THE OPEN ROAD

Shut the shack door,
packed the car, and
drove to San Francisco
400 miles through valleys of larks —

      the hills that year so green a
      sheen of gold cast over them,
      as if the eye just couldn't
      stand such green

         and not a single Poppy!
         State Flower
         spookily gone

But I don't care in my Survival Car when
O, my Lady loves to ride with me!

       hot whiskey
       long concrete
       back seat
       rifle food & sleeping bag

Motionless, finally, finally just
drifting along on concrete belt going
70-miles-an-hour underneath my car
Still, except for the swing of the steering wheel, and
She!
my Lady loves to sing to me!

       anarchist lectures 5 hours long,
       songs all winter wrong set right

(and won't even let me stop to scribble them down)

Hot
Whiskey

Long concrete

Big Chevvy Engine 6-Ply Song how

Shrineless, I

pilgrim

       through the world

HE FINALLY REACHES THE CITY

Woke up sick and old, in somebody else's bed

      "somewhere in the Universe"

to a glass of orange juice, a note

          (how she had to go to work and what
          the phone and when,

                Gloria X X X)

          Celsus?   Day?   O!

Warm glass of water in the bathroom strange towels
bottles, goo. Ubiquitous
crazy razor hopeless lady-blades

          "I don't know who you are, but
          I'm going to shave you anyway."

Diet pills in the medicine chest!

          (terrible vision of hyped-up ladies
          much too skinny anyway Amphetamine
          suburb babble!

          Nowhere? Nowhere, anymore, that
          fat & lovely Mother-Flesh to
          lay our heads upon

          "There there, Lewie," nursely.
          almost unconcerned

          as if her flesh were there
          to give a rest to
          new flesh, thinner,
          growing, and
          sometimes scared . . .

kids fidgety in the suburbs

the Mothers "Handsome")

Check the milligrams, take the necessary dose
Forward! Into Day!

Damp, towel about my loins,
back to scented room, to
orange juice, to
Miracle!
        (2 full inches left of Vodka)

Is this, then, the
Mystical Return? The
Man come back?

        The Red Monk used to say:

        Find yourself at some ridiculous task,
        say, urinating in the hostess's flower bed,
        the party raging on, above,

        and imagine all your life, and past lives,
        till you see them vividly. Then,

        shaking off the dew, say out loud:

        So,
        It has all come to this?

On with the groovy boots.
On with essential shades against the glare

　　　　(remembering Lamantia's poem

　　　　　　　Blue Grace
　　　　　　　behind dark glasses

　　　　　　　Steps out of a
　　　　　　　hundred white cars

　　　　　　　all over town . . .

How clean it looked, that walked out through the door!

　　　Ah City!

　　　　　　　I would tell you how it was to

　　　stalk your streets!

　　So young!　　　*Anonymous!*

HE LOCATES THE LIVE MUSEUM

*For Kirby Doyle, remembering his house
in Larkspur*

Finally there's no room for it all. Masterpieces lean face
against the wall, and the trail on up to it is littered with sculpture.
Mushrooms grow in a Theater for Artaud.

And you can't put your hand down, even accidentally,
without it coming back with a treasure in it—some flake off the
Planet, or a spooky little box.

When you open the door, it's funky-beaded, feathered, and
white.

Wine! How beautiful! We were almost out of wine!

Has anybody ever said, out loud, that our job is to give ourselves
away? That now and then we must have rest from that work? That
this is the resting place?

The Mountain Man returns. The soldier returns. The shy
inhabiter of rooms, returns. The husband returns. The frightened
girl. The boy who cannot tell, just yet, how right he is.

Embracing. Everyone embracing.

Where we show us what we made in solitude. Where we tell
us everything we know.

Where we catch our breath, and weep.

We sit on each others laps and look into our eyes, where the
dancer who is actually a fawn plays flute and the girls, who are all
of them sisters, sing and sew.

We are "drows'd," as Keats used to say, "by the fume of
poppies."

It's hard to understand Collectors. Impossible to make them see it's made and made and made and can't be kept. I drink to them. I smoke to them. I pity them. I've given up. I cannot ever share my bliss.

Coffee in a shaky cup.

Crash of last night's bottles in the garbage pit.

Bedding aired and put away the
girls, now, plaiting each other's hair and
painting on their eyes, and

Look, Lewie,

Here comes another one!

all of us sharing Wonder as it breaks again across our hills

the Sun

HE BEGINS TO RECOUNT HIS ADVENTURES

I can't remember seeing it any other way but whole, a big round rock wheeling about the heavens and comin' on green to crack sidewalks, gentle and undemanding, as if I saw it first, approaching it from somewhere else.

Everything about it always seemed right. The roundness is right. The way it spins.

I used to wonder why you couldn't break every speed record just by going straight up and somehow hang up there awhile, while the world spun around beneath you.

Suppose you dug a tunnel all the way to China and then jumped into the hole. You'd fall down through the center, and then fall up — almost to the other side. Then you'd fall back down again, up again, down again, each time losing a little distance, till finally you'd be hanging there, exactly in the middle — the only place in the world where every way is up.

Somebody said it's way too hot in there and nobody could possibly do it. Others thought I'd shoot out way up over China and then fall back and miss the hole ('cause the world would turn a little in the meantime) and just end up killing my damn fool self.

But I liked the part at the very end, when you're falling only 50 feet or so, through and back and through again, like a very slow kind of floating quiver or something.

You could bounce on it, later, or even walk around on it (in it, through it). You keep going *through* it all the time. Like those dolls with weighted bottoms only you don't ever have a table top to end up right side up on. A weird bouncy sort of spin thing you couldn't ever get out of. You could try, but you'd never make it: 3,959 miles straight up in all directions.

All the colors are right. We say it's mostly green and blue, but other animals see it differently than that and when you get up high enough it all gets black, so maybe it's just our eyes that make the colors right.

The balance of land and water is right — a very good thing in a spinning ball. If too much weight were on one side it'd shake itself to pieces, or get into some wacky eccentric extra orbit kind thing — worse and worse till finally it all breaks loose from the Sun's pull and wings on out into nowhere, crashing into planets and suns and generally causing all kinds of unimaginable hassles and disasters.

Not only is the land and water balanced right, the shapes are very beautiful. The two big land-shapes are strikingly similar, for example, and right. They both have narrow places near the middle — the right place to be narrow.

Everything is right, clear down to the smallest parts of it. I know a beach that's made up entirely of little round stones the size of a pea or smaller. All smooth and round little pieces of jade, jasper, agate, moonstones, glass from broken bottles, shells, tiny pieces of wood — and you get so hung up in a few square yards you just can't stop collecting and hunting and looking into it and suddenly there's an unbelievably tiny little pure white claw of a crab and *on that* is something even smaller, crawling!

Even smaller than that, it's right. You can spend your whole life looking through microscopes at subworlds living off further subworlds, just as surely as looking through a telescope at light years and light years of worlds so far away they aren't even there anymore — nothing's there except this little blip of light that finally travelled far enough to hit your human eyeball and live, thereby. The whole thing finally coming together as Rexroth said: . . . "like looking at a drop of ink and suddenly finding you're looking at the Milky Way."

Or John Muir waking in a Sierra meadow, in spring, and finding, inches from his waking eye, a wildflower he, and nobody else, had ever seen. Rising, he found himself in a field of delicate color so complicated he spent the whole day in only ten square feet of it, classifying and drawing pictures of hundreds of little plants for the first time in the world.

An average of a ton of insects for every acre of a field like that. Deer-hoof crushing a flower. Rodents at the roots of it. Birds diving and pecking at it. Big trees crowding it out with their shade. Mushrooms in the warm fall rains.

Ridges rising into mountains and air too thin and not much dirt for it. Shy little Coneys nibbling at tiny moss. Snow and Glaciers and the peaks at last.

Eternal snow where no matter how far up it is you can bet your life some man, sometime, stood, and looked, and wept again for wonder of this Human eye!

HE EXPLAINS IT ANOTHER WAY

•

At times we're almost able to see it was once all

Light, and wants to get back to it.

Not brilliant, swift, or huge, since Light

is the measure, and we are

Flake off of All-Measure

Cinder cast down from Sun

(explaining every "fall" and why we yearn so?)

Harnessed jelly of the Stars!

•

BOOK IV

(1964 – 1968)

DIN POEM, COURSES

DIN POEM

Tizuvthee, Old Soapy, land where Thoreau sat and Whitman
walked, despised of all nations, Strontium, alone

Tizuvthee

Fucked L.A. starlet of tiny dream untrue even to your
        tiny dream intolerable up-tight dirty noise New
        York, rusty muscle Chicago, hopeless Cleveland
        Akron Visalia alcoholic San Francisco suicide

Tizuvthee, I sing

SUPERMARKET SONG

Super Anahist cough syrup tastes as good as the syrup they put
    on ice cream.
Super Anahist cough syrup tastes as good as the syrup they put
    on ice cream.
Super Anahist cough syrup tastes as good as the syrup they put
    on ice cream.

        Let's take out the car and park it
        at the big new super market
        and go on inside and see
        what they got for you and me.

        Look at all the brand names!
        Aren't they really grand names!
        Continental Can Corporation of America
        has arranged that to be!

        Pepsi Cola, Coca-Cola,
        Rice Crispies & Del Monte
        Best Foods! Best Foods! Best Foods!

116

Everything is wrapped in plastic.
Everything begins to look like it came from L.A.
and they/deal out the pineapple Dole/
to better enable you to meet your role

as customer
of the big new super market
where we take our car and we park it,

and bread will never rot
and you've got to

Save the stamps!
Save the stamps!

Save the stamps
it's fun.

Hi Man, what's happening. See you people later.
Hi Man, what's happening. See you people later.
Hi Man, what's happening. See you people later.

Lowering the butterfat
to meet marketing requirements
actually increases the
percentage of Calcium,
Potassium, Phosphorous,
and other food elements

You could make this marriage work if you'd only try!

I am in Personnel.

Anti-personnel bomb. Exceptional Children. Homogenized.
Over-kill. Hydrogenated. Apostolic Faith. Pentecostal.

He died for our sins.

Pentecostal holy-mission. United Brotherhood of the Sons of Father Baptism Apostolic. Virgin Mother house of Grace the holy ghost immersion. Sanctuary redemption. Death. Devil finds work for idle excommunicate. Confess thy total pentecostal immersion, my son.

I pledge allegiance.

You never say you love me anymore.

NEVER. NEVER PUT THE GOD-DAMN CAMERA IN THE GLOVE COMPARTMENT. I TOLD YOU AND TOLD YOU TO NEVER PUT THE GOD-DAMN CAMERA IN THE GLOVE COMPARTMENT. SO WHAT DO YOU DO? YOU PUT THE GOD-DAMN CAMERA IN THE GLOVE COMPARTMENT. AND IT'S STOLEN! SEE?

Nigger.
Nigger town.

Nigger car. Nigger suit. Gypsy.

Nigger gypsy poet wop. Jew.

Spic.

Nigger gypsy poet wop beatnic. Spic wop. Wop wop.

Jew nigger beatnic poet wop spic commie. Beat commie. Poet commie. Faggot wop. Nigger.

Nigger house. Nigger fence. Nigger poet beatnic wop.

Wop wop. Dope fiend.

Dope fiend nigger. Yellah nigger. Nigger lovin' beatnic wop. Nigger.

Ashtray nigger. Billboard nigger. Nigger wall nigger suit nigger shoes nigger.

Nigger nigger.

Sunset.

Flower.

Nigger flower

The Christmas message carries a great and wondrous hope.
This hope, advanced with courage and determination, is a
very present help to you and to your doctors and nurses.
As they assist you in your effort for full recovery to
health, you can count upon the continuing gratitude and
concern of your fellow Americans.

Dwight D. Eisenhower

> If I told you once,
> I told you a thousand times

All right fella!

Where's your I.D.?

How long you lived at that address?

Get in the car.

"I don't know what's the matter honey, I'm not always this
way."

"Oh baby, that's all right, the sex thing is only a part
of it."

"Yeah but I want you so bad and the damned thing . . .

"Ahh, don't worry about it, please, the sex thing . . ."

"I'm perfectly all right and then I try to roll on top
and the god damn thing . . ."

"Shhh. Shhh. Don't. I mean it, really, it's all right.
Really baby. The sex thing's only a little part of it and . . ."

Here kitty kitty. Here kitty kitty kitty. Where's that damn cat
anyway. Kitty? Here kitty kitty. Here you god damn kitty kitty . . .

Apostolic Faith Mission Love in Christ of God Salvation gave his
life for YOU in virgin house of love lady in
Christ BEHOLDEN and KNOW, *Believe* on his words better to
avoid the bait of sin than STRUGGLE on the hook, beholden,
hope. Nameless name IMMACULATE yearning for him
DAUGHTERS of sin beholden and NOT ASKED before his
THRONE!

You've been late four times this month.

Jiveassmuthafucka, Javassmuthafucka

Jive.   Ass.   Mother.   Fucker.

Chickens can't lay eggs unless there's a rooster around
can they?

What's that girl doing down the hall, anyway?

Where you workin' fella?   Get in the car.

Let's get him fixed. They're much nicer pets if you get 'em
fixed.

Do you still feel bad?

I am on top of the Empire State Building leaning on the railing which I have carefully examined to see if it's strongly made. The sound of it comes all that way, up, to me. A hum. Thousands of ventilators far away. Now and then I hear an improbable clank. The air, even up here, is warmed by it.

To the north a large green rectangle, Central Park, lies flat, clean-edged, indented. A skin has been pulled off, a bandage removed, and a small section of the Planet has been allowed to grow.

I think, "They have chosen to do this in order to save their lives." And then I think, "It is not really a section of the Planet, it is a perfect imitation of a section of the Planet (remembering the zoo). It is how they think it might look." I am struck by their wisdom. Moved.

The elevator is not too crowded. We are all silent and perfectly behaved, except a little girl who is whispering something to her mother. Her mother holds her hand and bends down to listen. The little girl giggles. Hunching her shoulders and screwing up her face. She has told her mother something outrageous.

In the lobby are people who are really doing it, not like us, just looking around. They wear the current costume and read the office directories beside the banks and banks of elevators. I realize there are offices in the Empire State Building! It is not just a tower to look from!

It all starts coming in, on the street. Each one is going somewhere, thinking. Many are moving their lips, talking to themselves. In 2 blocks I am walking as fast as they are. We all agree to wait when the light turns red.

In the subway it is more intense. Something about being *under* the ground? It is horrifying to let it all come in, in the subway.

A small Jew with crazed eyes and a little bent old body is carrying a shopping bag and is wearing two brown vests. He has, for a walking stick, a length of curtain rod, solid brass. He avoids a post and doesn't look into the large trash-basket. His lips are moving.

A gust of dirty air hits me as I rise out of it at the 7th Ave. subway exit. I am relieved, perhaps because the buildings are lower, the street wider, the intersection a jumble of crazy angles?

The white walls of an apartment generously lent by a girl I hardly know. She moved up to the Bronx, to her mother's, just to give us a place to stay. I lock the doors and think how perfect an apartment it is.

The top of the brandy bottle is correctly designed. I don't have to fuss with a difficult plastic seal. All I have to do is twist it off.

Outside, a ventilator randomly clanks . . . . .

•

Years ago, somewhere inconceivably else, I could have been given a strange assignment.

He was a short man, gray haired but mostly bald. He explained the thing to me in a homey kind of office.

"I can fix you up to be, actually *be,* a Native of a World!" he said. "You won't be *like* them, you will *be* one of them. Think the way they do, see as they see etc. *with exactly their physical and mental equipment.* You can see, of course, what this means! It means your data, for the first time, will be absolutely accurate. You will, in every sense, *know* what it is to be one."

I have forgotten all he said about the reports I'd have to make on my return, but I can almost remember the taste of the potion I got. Brassy, but not too bad.

And what is happening during moments like that on the Empire State building is simply that the potion's effect is flickering out. There are moments of wakefulness, and it all starts coming in.

You see it on the faces of the others. They are all more or less drugged. Many are as straight or straighter than you are, but are pretending not to be. As you are pretending not to be.

It is then, while watching the ones who are actually doing it (not like us, just looking around), that you realize there are *only* people more or less drugged into this vast, insane, assignment.

There are no natives!

I pledge allegiance to the Pentecostal Brotherhood of the Faith in. I never felt worse. Do you still feel bad? How long have you lived at that address? Get in the car.

I've never been so ashamed in my life.

You don't know how much better I feel. It's like having some beautiful thing protecting you all the time. A soft and lovely power that's devoted only to good. Get in the car.

"It's called Conation and Affect."

Exceptional Children. Anti-Personnel Bomb. Top Secret.

"What kind of books does he read?"

I told you a thousand times.

It is better not to marry but it is better to marry than to burn. Water seeks its own level.

You've been late four times this month.

You could make this marriage work if you'd only try

Adieu, adieu

Soleil cou coupe

Meadowlark

Dove

COURSES

No Credit No Blame No Balm

COURSE COLLEGE CREDO

We refuse the right to serve anybody.

GEOGRAPHY

The Far East is west of us,
nearer by far
than the Near East,
and mysteriouser.

Is the Middle East
really the Middle West?

And there aren't 7 continents,
there are 6—

Europe and Asia are
stuck together

in the middle.

HISTORY

Every 30 years or so, Elders arm Children
with expensive weapons and send them away
to kill other children similarly armed.

Some do not return. Some return
maimed or terrified into madness.
Many come back brutal.

Nothing else changes.

Mr. Krupp got the whole works back
by producing a single document

from his briefcase.

AESTHETICS

Not very many can do it really well.

Nobody knows why.

MATH

One and one makes two. There is a
two which is one,
at last. One alone is lonely.

Three is possible.
There are plenty of holes for everybody.

Four is nearly impossible.
Try it.

A great mathematician
(and this is a true story),
while waiting in a brothel and
looking at dirty pictures,

suddenly got the vision of
all the combinations of all the
plugs and holes of Nine.

Excited, he ran home and invented our
theorems of combinations and permutations.

That day, he didn't get laid.

THEOLOGY

The True Rebel never advertises it,

He prefers His joy to Missionary Work.

Church is Bureaucracy,
no more interesting than any Post Office.

Religion is Revelation:
all the Wonder of all the Planets striking
all your Only Mind.

Guard the Mysteries!
Constantly reveal Them!

PSYCHOLOGY

The trouble is
most people spend their lives living it

down.

BOTANY

Consider the Passion Flower:

Who'd ever think a plant would go to
so much trouble

just to get fucked
by a Bee.

PHILOSOPHY

Never ask Why What,
Always ask What's What.
Observe, connect, and do.

The great Winemaster is almost a
magician to the bulk of his Tribe,
to his Peers he is only accurate.

"He knows the Grape so well," they say,

"He turned into a Vine."

THE BASIC CON

Those who can't find anything to live for,
always invent something to die for.

Then they want the rest of us to
die for it, too.

These, and an elite army of thousands,
who do nobody any good at all, but do
great harm to some,
have always collected vast sums from all.

Finally, all this machinery
tries to kill us,

because we won't die for it, too.

COURSE COLLEGE GRADUATION ADDRESS

(1) Freak out.
(2) Come back.
(3) Bandage the wounded and feed
    however many you can.
(4) Never cheat.

COURSE COLLEGE OATH

All persecutors
Shall be violated!

BOOK V

(1969 – 1971)

THE SONG
MT. TAMALPAIS SINGS

THE SONG MT. TAMALPAIS SINGS

This is the last place. There is nowhere else to go.

>Human movements,
>>but for a few,
>are Westerly.
>Man follows the Sun.

This is the last place. There is nowhere else to go.

>Or follows what he thinks to be the
>movement of the Sun.
>It is hard to feel it, as a rider,
>on a spinning ball.

This is the last place. There is nowhere else to go.

>Centuries and hordes of us,
>from every quarter of the earth,
>now piling up,
>and each wave going back
>to get some more.

This is the last place. There is nowhere else to go.

>"My face is the map of the Steppes,"
>she said, on this mountain, looking West.

>My blood set singing by it,
>to the old tunes,
>Irish, still,
>among these Oaks.

This is the last place. There is nowhere else to go.

This is why
once again we celebrate
the great Spring Tides.

Beaches are strewn again with Jasper,
Agate, and Jade.
The Mussel-rock stands clear.

This is the last place. There is nowhere else to go.

This is why
once again we celebrate the
Headland's huge, cairn-studded, fall
into the Sea.

This is the last place. There is nowhere else to go.

For we have walked the jeweled beaches
at the feet of the final cliffs
of all Man's wanderings.

This is the last place.
There is nowhere else we need to go.

OLEMA SATORI

for Peter Coyote

Walking from the gate to the farmhouse,

Buzzards wheeling close as 20 feet,
to the West a ridge of
redwoods, fir, that
goofy Pt. Reyes pine,

walking on a dirt farm road,

small birds darting from the grass,
cows, burnt hills,
tongue of the Pacific,
ridge and the Last Ocean,
my boots,
walking,

"This is all you get,"
Olema said.

And I said, "That's
twice as much as I could ever hope for."

And Peter said,

"You can have the whole thing,
with fur covered pillows,

at the same price."

SAUSALITO TRASH PRAYER

Sausalito,
  Little Willow,
Perfect Beach by the last Bay in the world,
  None more beautiful,

    Today we kneel at thy feet
    And curse the men who have misused you.

PRAYER TO A MOUNTAIN SPRING

Gentle Goddess,

Who never asks for anything at all,
and gives us everything we have,

thank you for this sweet water,

and your fragrance.

THE RIDDLE OF HANDS

In every culture, in every place and time, there has always been a religion, and in every one of these religions there has always been the gesture of hands clasped together, as Christians do to pray, in order to signify something important.

Why is this?

(There is only one right answer to this riddle)

COMMENTARY BY THE RED MONK

The gesture has but one source. Who would think to pick his nose, or cross his eyes, at such a moment?
The man who claims to feel power between his hands is lost in forms and ideas. The man who clasps his hands and waits will never see the light.

THE RIDDLE OF BOWING

In every culture, in every place and time, there has always been a religion, and in every one of these religions there has always been the gesture of bowing so fully that the forehead strikes the ground.

Why is this?

(There is only one right answer to this riddle)

COMMENTARY BY THE RED MONK

Sooner or later the gesture is necessary no matter which way you go. Suzuki bows with so much confidence we all feel bold.

Author's Note:

The Riddle of Hands and the Riddle of Bowing are real riddles. There is only one right answer to Hands and one, different, right answer to Bowing. They are the first American Koans. They are Koans for beginners, making no claims for Perfect Enlightenment, but those who solve them will discover a deep spiritual insight.

It is no accident that people, everywhere, have always clasped their hands that way, for those purposes. Think about it. Why not any of the millions of other gestures and stances? Why, always, this one?

It took me 3 1/2 years to solve the question after the question occurred to me. It isn't easy. It's so simple it is almost unavailable to our crooked heads.

The Riddle of Bowing is much the easier of the two. Try that first and use the same Mind to try to solve Hands.

Anyone who solves the Riddles may get the answer confirmed by writing me through *Coyote*.* But please don't waste my time by telling me that Bowing shows respect for the earth or that you are vunerable to a great power or you are submitting to something. I haven't got time for that baby-talk.

* This Author's Note was published in *Coyote's Journal #9*, 1971. Ed.

THE RIDER RIDDLE

If you spend as much time on the Mountain as you should, She will always give you a Sentient Being to ride: animal, plant, insect, reptile, or any of the Numberless Forms.

What do *you* ride?

(There is one right answer for every person, and only that person can really know what it is)

COMMENTARY BY THE RED MONK

Manjusri rode a tiger. One, just as fierce as he, rode a mouse. There is no one who can tell you what the answer is. The Mountain will show you.

REDWOOD HAIKU

Orange, the brilliant slug —
Nibbling at the leaves of
Trillium

DIFFICULTY ALONG THE WAY

Seeking Perfect Total Enlightenment
is looking for a flashlight
when all you need the flashlight for
is to find your flashlight

WARNING OF TAMALPAIS

Let all quick-eyed, pride-full girls
take note of this

and every willing, head-strong boy
beware:

Nothing, in all the Universe, is more
sickening to see
than a good man, trying, and he

plagued by a bad woman!

SPRINGTIME IN THE ROCKIES, LICHEN

All these years I overlooked them in the
racket of the rest, this
symbiotic splash of plant and fungus feeding
on rock, on sun, a little moisture, air —
tiny acid-factories dissolving
salt from living rocks and
eating them.

Here they are, blooming!
Trail rock, talus and scree, all dusted with it:
rust, ivory, brilliant yellow-green, and
cliffs like murals!
Huge panels streaked and patched, quietly
with shooting-stars and lupine at the base.

Closer, with the glass, a city of cups!
Clumps of mushrooms and where do the
plants begin? Why are they doing this?
In this big sky and all around me peaks &
the melting glaciers, why am I made to
kneel and peer at Tiny?

These are the stamps on the final envelope.

How can the poisons reach them?
In such thin air, how can they care for the
loss of a million breaths?
What, possibly, could make their ground more bare?

Let it all die.

The hushed globe will wait and wait for
what is now so small and slow to
open it again.

As now, indeed, it opens it again, this
scentless velvet,
crumbler-of-the-rocks,

this Lichen!

SONG OF THE TURKEY BUZZARD

For Rock Scully
who heard it
the first
time

Praises, Tamalpais,
*   Perfect in Wisdom and Beauty,*
She of the Wheeling Birds

I.

The rider riddle is easy to ask,
but the answer might surprise you.

How desperately I wanted Cougar
(I, Leo, etc.)
                brilliant proofs: terrain,
color, food, all
nonsense. All made up.

They were always there, the
laziest high-flyers, bronze-winged,
the silent ones

"A cunning man always laughs and smiles,
        even if he's desperately hungry,
while a good bird always flies like a vulture,
        even if it is starving."

(Milarepa sang)

Over and over again, that sign:

I hit one once, with a .22
heard the "flak" and a feather flew off, he
flapped his wings just once and
went on sailing. Bronze

(when seen from above)

> as I have seen them, all day sitting
> on a cliff so steep they
> circled below me, in the up-draft
> passed so close I could see his
> eye.

Praises, Tamalpais,
  Perfect in Wisdom and Beauty,
She of the Wheeling Birds

Another time the vision was so clear another saw it, too. Wet, a hatching bird, the shell of the egg streaked with dry scum, exhausted, wet, too weak to move the shriveled wings, fierce sun-heat, sand. Twitching, as with elbows (we all have the same parts). Beak open, neck stretched, gasping for air. O how we want to live!

"Poor little bird," she said, "he'll never make it."

Praises, Tamalpais,
  Perfect in Wisdom and Beauty,
She of the Wheeling Birds

Even so, I didn't get it for a long long while. It finally came in a trance, a coma, half in sleep and half in fever-mind. A Turkey Buzzard, wounded, found by a rock on the mountain. He wanted to die alone. I had never seen one, wild, so close. When I reached out, he sidled away, head drooping, as dizzy as I was. I put my hands on his wing-shoulders and lifted him. He tried, feebly, to tear at my hands with his beak. He tore my flesh too slightly to make any difference. Then he tried to heave his great wings. Weak as he was, I could barely hold him.

A drunken veterinarian found a festering bullet in his side, a .22 that slid between the great bronze scales his feathers were. We removed it and cleansed the wound.

Finally he ate the rotten gophers I trapped and prepared for him. Even at first, he drank a lot of water. My dog seemed frightened of him.

They smell sweet
    meat is dry on their talons

The very opposite of
    death

bird of re-birth
    Buzzard

meat is rotten meat made
    sweet again and

lean, unkillable, wing-locked
    soarer till he's but a

speck in the highest sky
    infallible

eye finds Feast! on
    baked concrete

    free!

squashed rabbit ripened:
    our good cheese

(to keep the highways clean, and bother no Being)

II.

Praises Gentle Tamalpais
Perfect in Wisdom and Beauty of the
sweetest water
and the soaring birds

great seas at the feet of thy cliffs

Hear my last Will & Testament:

Among my friends there shall always be
one with proper instructions
for my continuance.

Let no one grieve.
I shall have used it all up
used up every bit of it.

What an extravagance!
What a relief!

On a marked rock, following his orders,
place my meat.

All care must be taken not to
frighten the natives of this
barbarous land, who
will not let us die, even,
as we wish.

With proper ceremony disembowel what I no longer need, that it
might more quickly rot and tempt

my new form

NOT THE BRONZE CASKET BUT THE BRAZEN WING

SOARING FOREVER ABOVE THEE O PERFECT

O SWEETEST WATER O GLORIOUS

WHEELING

BIRD

UNCOLLECTED POEMS

EDITOR'S NOTE

By the fall of 1969 Lew Welch had completed assembling, from
the work of two decades, his collected poems, which he called
Ring of Bone after a *Hermit Poem* based on a vision that had come
to him in a cabin in Bixby Canyon, Big Sur, in 1962. During the
next few months he finished writing his Preface, added several
more early poems to the "On Out" section, and completed, at last,
"The Way Back" poems, a sequence he had first drafted in 1963.
By February of 1970 the book had been accepted by a New York
publisher, a contract signed, and an advance on royalties paid. All
seemed fair sailing for Lew Welch and his book.

Alas, such was not to be. Storm clouds soon gathered and
publication of the book was many times postponed. Then when
Lew Welch walked away in May of 1971 he left a farewell note
naming me his literary executor and directing me to use not only
his assembled *Ring of Bone* manuscript but all of his papers as well.
In other words, he must have been thinking of a larger collection
that would include more poems from all periods of his life. The
contract lapsed in 1972, as he had anticipated, and I assumed the
final editing and publication of his collected poems.

After a careful study of his mss and correspondence,
particularly with fellow poets Gary Snyder and Philip Whalen,
I came to the conclusion that what was needed, in the present,
much changed situation was a more extensive collection than Lew
Welch had conceived of in 1969. To that end I have assembled in
the following pages a large number of uncollected poems from the
two decades of work, as they have survived in literary magazines,
as broadsides and free poems, in manuscripts and in letters. These
include not only late poems that he clearly intended to publish
in subsequent volumes, but also poems from all periods which
he had left out of *Ring of Bone,* perhaps because he felt they were
not "exactly accurate" (his phrase), or were incompletely realized,
or were too naive, sentimental, fragmentary, unfinished or did
not allow themselves to be "organized into" the structure he had
established, as he describes it in his Preface. Yet all these poems
possess considerable interest.

The first two — "The Importance of Autumn" and
"Monologue of One Whom the Spring Found Unaccompanied"
— are the first poems Welch published (in 1950 issues of *Janus,*
the Reed College literary magazine of the period). Several are

fragments cannibalized from long philosophical poems he worked on at various times but never completed to his satisfaction. "Invention Against Invention," as an example, is a long poem describing the events of a day in 1960 San Francisco from which he carved two of the "Four Studies in Perception" and "Entire Sermon by the Red Monk" as well; I have included it as a fascinating example of a long poem in progress and for what was *not* rescued from it. "Small Book to Break the Brain" appears to have been designed originally to include "all the Leo Poems and all the Sermons and commentaries by the Red Monk"; but presumably this project was abandoned. The "Three Songs in Rat Flat" did not survive final translation into *Hermit Poems*. Clifford Burke tells me Welch referred to "Law" and "Comportment" as "Postgraduate Courses." Other poems explore the possibilities of new forms in poetry.

In May of 1970, during a stop in Salt Lake City, he drafted the contents and wrote a little preface for a new book he planned to call "Cement." (He seems to have forgotten that he had already incorporated "Small Sentence to Drive Yourself Sane" in "He Finally Reaches the City.") I have been able to find and assemble all the poems he proposed to include except for these three:

> Suicide .38 Story
> On the Loss of Magda's Teeth
> Pigeons and Puke

Another list, on a bar napkin, gives these under the heading "To Write":

> 40th Birthday
> Dragon Fly (Birth)
> The Docks, 1970
> The Turn
> The Last Mussel-Feast, A Curse
> The Uses of Poetry
> Big Sur

An early poem titled "The Uses of Poetry" is included in this volume; perhaps Welch intended to revise it once more. "Big Sur" might mean he planned to develop a poem from the long letter to Robert Duncan he drafted in 1962 and never sent. These poems, and no doubt others, were either never written down or are lost. Hopefully they and other lost poems will turn up in time.

Many people have freely given valuable assistance to the preparation of this volume. I am particularly grateful to Magda Cregg, Dr. Dorothy Brownfield, and equally to Gary Snyder and Philip Whalen, and to Norman H. Davis, Lew Welch's bibliographer, for their advice at crucial steps along the way. Three librarians have given most useful aid: Martha Berqquist and Luella R. Pollock of the Reed College Library, and Julian Michel of the University of California (Berkeley) Library. I am also much indebted to these fellow poets and friends of the poet: Clifford Burke, Frank Dietrich, Tony Dingman, Bob Durand, Valerie Estes, Mary Norbert Körte, Dan Mathews, Stan Rice, Grover Sales, Jack Shoemaker, Charles Upton and Bill Yardas.

Donald Allen
Bolinas 1973/1976

THE IMPORTANCE OF AUTUMN

when that autumnal wind
busy with the rubbish of a year
divests the tree of lingering ornaments
sending them whirling with the fallen ones

when that consumptive flush
that culmination
pretense
fragmentation
reveals a tree of sticks
that cannot cage the wind

and ducks pass black and low
in a sky of so intense a glare
that gulls seem gray

then look closely

for in this primal light

you'll see love walking
with the wind pressed to her thighs

you'll see her as she dances
dancing counter to the whirling leaves

you'll see her dance 'til suddenly she
stops
quieting the leaves

some settle on her breast and hair
one floats by — she
hits it with her hand

and vanishes

then on a field of dark pine trees
burst flocks of gulls
white

[1949-50]

MONOLOGUE OF ONE WHOM THE SPRING FOUND UNACCOMPANIED

It happens, at times,
That the route becomes beautiful
The incline gentle and the landscape rich
And on the heavy air the smell of growing things

We think the secret hidden in the land
Or month or year
Or traced upon the chart by which we go,
But do not tinker so with subtleties

You brush the secret with your hand,
As the arm swings, striding.

Gone, you'll know how much more real her absence is
With sound of her that's missing now in every sound
With walk of her that's missing now in every passer-by

Who speaks incessantly
Speaks of how the buds unfold
Of how these days the twigs are fat
Of how all things begin to bloom

How every god-damned thing begins to bloom.

[1950]

BREAKFAST, ONE EASTER

Cardinal,
         Masked and mitred bird,
Your scarlet,
Perched on tines of a newly rusted rake,
         Made Easter, Easter's sun.

And we who made blood sacrifice,
Once, on another hillside,
         Robed in another red,
Awoke beside a lake less blue than we supposed,
         Under a sun less warm,
And broke the winter's fast with April's eggs.

All about us wings,
         And scarlet wings.

SWEET DEATH

for Gavin

How can I come to pity
Not despise
Those who themselves deprive
Of this sweet death

When I myself at times
Should Love burst in the room
Skitter sideways to the wall
Crab with a lifted claw

ANECDOTE OF TANGERINES

I with fifteen cents to spend
would make a gift of tangerines

walked
47 blocks and back
where they were cheap enough
with 8 fruit bought from the man with a cart
at Paddy's market

so cold it was that day
that when an old lady
lifting up her veil
spit
the spittle on the sidewalk steamed

the son of a bitch slipped 4 spoiled ones in
and the girl phoned up
breaking the date

so I ate them
the 4 remaining tangerines
section by section
alone in my room
spitting the seeds into a dish

they were
sweet

[1950?]

OLYMPIA OYSTERS

Olympia oysters
small as lima beans
36 of them
raw

squeeze on each one one
drop of lemon juice
(no more)

a speck of sauce upon the tines then
spear the naked things!

the flavor eludes now now
blooms within the mouth

36 of them
raw

[1950]

NOT THIS GRADUAL INTELLIGENCE

The rite should be performed with real knives
I, with hickory-knot between my teeth, bearing an obvious pain
While girls (to be admired) admire
And clay, red clay, is plastered on my head.

All the women keening
All the birds crying as they wheel above our heads
And the wet dance of the elders:
Suck of their bare pads lifting from the purpled mud.

Finally an emblem:
Feather from the wing of some
Rare and scarlet bird for me to wear
Ostentatiously.

Rite and the real knife
Not this gradual intelligence.

[1950]

THE USES OF POETRY

For centuries girls have been seduced by poetry.
They like it.
All those words slamming at their
navel, neck, and knees:
parts of their loveliness they never bothered to see.

Looking down, they agree, become
conscious of elbows, ankles, earlobes etc.,
discover that the belly has begun to buzz.

Moist, they turn to us and are
made, thereby, immortal.

And we?
Without her, what is there to say,
or do?

[1950?]

UTENSIL

given to me by neighbor George, the old man:
spoon

plain with "Linton's" pressed on handle tip
over this (rudely forc'd) "H & H Co"
the Automat

Linton's the Automat then George
copped it, kept it awhile
then gave it to me

the concave surface of its business end
has many tiny nicks
dents like those the grass will make
on naked thighs

of sturdier metal
plated with silver
spoon
a table
spoon

[1950?]

THE EPIPHANY OF TOFFY BELSKY

eyes looking straight into my eyes
"take me with you"
she said
and I did

to the basement cafeteria
unfortunately
where we sneaked a cup of coffee
on company time

the eyes too
but mostly that voice
female
blending perfectly question and demand
saying

"take me with you"

[1950]

DAVID IS DEAD

David who in those days
Stood upon pounded sand and
Scratched through banks of shale
For one round stone,
David who in those days looked to the sea
Is dead.

That rock he watched,
That tower at the sea's edge,
Lost its chance to lurch,
Lift, in clouds of gulls,
And stride,
Weed
Slapping at its thigh.

That rock he watched
Will be a roost for gulls.
And here is a bit of drift.
And over there a crab,
Suds at his mouth,
Is clicking the stem of his eye.

[1951]

EPITHALAMION

Never in our long history did steam-flanked
Bull come shambling down its mountainside or
Miracle seek Lap of Innocence

But Poet, Painter, Architect, the
Lost and the nascent Great besiege
Until time ripen for the choosing and
The choice of such as she.

That from her golden patch should spring
A race to make all Hectors pale and
Helen but a partial dream . . . rude

Bone and Brain and Eye to make
The vision swim as now
Our vision swims us

Half in dream and
Half beneath reality.

[1955]

COMPLEYNT OF HIS MISTRESS

Lately Tulip genders her
And chastely closes on the night.

Field Worm draws himself below
Rabbit hides and Owl takes flight.

Mass burrowing.
Stubble washed by Moon not quite

So cold as you'd suppose.
Laugh at the Moon old man.

Compose.

[1955]

WORDS TO THAT EFFECT

I spend most my time inside my head
There's a use for it

            like now I think of
            cedar shutters and the
            spring wind fluttering
            them   .   smell of roses
            from the test gardens in
            Portland Oregon and

Here I am in Chicago
(not outside my head yet)

> naturally . how
> can you write a
> poem except from the
> inside out?

Last night I took a bath and couldn't even feel the heat.

> her magnificent breasts the
> total reality while my
> eyelids sweat and the picture
> coming through the holes in my
> eyes was that of my own thin
> shin-bones.

There! I was here
(just then)
She's standing by the window, looking at trees:

> "Isn't that a pretty young green?
> "The kind that people shouldn't wear?
> "Only the things that make it?

And I heard it!
(All the way down I mean.)
Anyway, *she* was here
(just before she told about it)

> I'm going to put my hands on both her tits
> and kiss her on the ear.

Where are you?
(Right now)
?

[1958]

A MATTER OF ORGAN STOPS AND STARTS

Consider the mind as an organ.
Set it so.

There is no other way than start and finish
and begin again and again. At least none that I know of
or have seen. One day they went westward and that was the
beginning. Now they go back and forth and there is no
beginning. It would not be so bad if they didn't want it
that way, but they do, they do, they do seem to want it
just that way.

Without small words.
Today.
Franklin was my friend but he was a bad speller.
Until today I had no wish for it.
Today I wish for it.

'Neath the spreading chestnut tree birds and
squirrels drink their tea. It is a very strong drink
for such little animals.

Together.
All together.
All all togetherness is and is was and it will
be exclusively.
That's an example of skittering.
It was and it is is exclusively.
Perhaps but not in this wind.
This is the wind that lets them think like that.
Underisive.
Indecisively and before they meant to like it.
It was and it was not done until long before that
anyway.
Where.

This kind of writing is done totally without recall
or recalling a syllable. One little word so nicely follows
the next one and then there will always be more and more of
them. It does not involve the mind I write from. It does
involve the way I pick out just that word and no other.
Naturally you have to change a word here and there but that
is long after you have already put all of it down.

Now I am writing from the mind I always write from.
With the slighest change of emphasis.
But not the mind Stein wrote from.

There. I am writing entirely from my mind.

[May 1957]

LARGE LITTLE CIRCLE

Recently I met a friend for the first time in 8 years

For 8 years he told his wife I said certain things which,
        all that time, I attributed to him

. . . some insight or other, more or less accurately phrased . . .

"WE'RE ALL THE SAME PERSON!"

Which is something another friend said. It's sometimes
        attributed to me.

[1957?]

SEVENTH GRADE

Grass,
by the sun burnt,
flecked as the throat of larks.

The grapes are pruned in Spanish fashion there.
Stumps, most of the year, a
fountain of tendrils in summer.

You had to reach way in underneath those leaves to
find grapes.
Mexicans picked them with curved knives.
Many were left to
sweeten in that tented heat.

I used to stop to pick them.
Heavy bunches swinging from my handlebars,
all the way to school.

One day Eagle came down from mountainside and
squatted on a phonepole.

[1957]

FOR JOSEPH KEPECS

The poem is not the heart's cry
(Though it seems to be if you have craft enough)
The poem is made to carry the heart's cry

And only to carry it. And the cry is always the
Same . . . for all times and every place the
Same perceptions met a hundred times, or once.

The rest is exhuberance.
The force left over after dealing with
An undemanding planet in a square time . . .

No more or less mysterious than the juicing
Of the glands. The need to skip a stone
Across that pond. To yell among high mountains.

You think you read for the heart's cry
But you do not. You read because no stone
Ever skips perfectly. Because that mountain

Always lets you down. Because no matter
How you yell the voice bounced back
is flat. The words are puny.

The need for another world that always works right
Is the heart's exhuberance.
We don't hide there. We spill over and

Make it.

[5/27/57]

175

NIGHTCLUB SCENE: 20/NOV/58

What is it?
Audience legitimately here as anywhere
Waiting
Actors legitimately here, too, I suppose,
Trying very hard

To do what?
              Waiting for what?

Is it for what I think?
The planet to be flipped
OVER (or on)?
              And they:
Trained to do it
Whatever it is

Almost happened when his
Fine-boned Spanish face broke down
              almost a matter of tissue dissolving
              reformed before the eyes

Mask gone
Instant of fierce dark face at precisely
ONE
With feet gone hooves and satyr-arch of back and
Raised arms really swift

Mind gone
Planet gone
Image of a person suddenly THERE

But where?
His dancing-space smaller than a card table
Light beams darting on him, thrown by
Hands and mind other than his and
Wrong

Where's the connection?
What's he tryin' to do?
What're we waiting for?

THERE HE GOES (I thought)

YAAH! (yelled)
mind where his went
gone somewhere

Something had to be added
WE were missing
(The meaning of "nowhere" in its useful sense)
And he?

GONE, almost
Effeminacy and mind-caress of lean Andalusian body gone
But . . .

It had to have firelight, ground,
Pounded clay, house partly
Cave, children . . .

And the next act worse:
Husky lady shrieking

"LOVE IS A
NURSERY RHYME."

Belting it
Like an Israeli battle call . . .

tough Jew-girl machine-gun

plain as a silver

ring.

FOR A KYGER KNOWN BY ANOTHER NAME

How did she get all the way up this hill
With one leg in a cast
On crutches
Dead drunk
In that very modern party dress
1:30 AM
Dirt trail treacherous with Eucalyptus nuts
The night moonless and fogged over anyway?

I knew a girl like that once. She said:

> "Sure. We read all of Sartre.
> The whole Philosophy class went over to
> Dr. G's house and we had six seminars on it.
> We decided he was only trying to say
> What everybody else was trying to say
> And he failed too."

Another girl I knew had a mouth just like that.
She played a game called "Squelch Welch" and
I went all the way to Aspen, Colorado for her once.

Thank God all that is over with . . .

> Come into the cabin
> And I will tell you
> All about Coleman stoves.

Perhaps we have some of that good cheese left.

[1958]

INVENTION AGAINST INVENTION

for Charles Olson

In the beautiful bathroom of a pederast I admire for other reasons:

> *How can we dismiss the needs of others,*
> *Having invented them?*

They are internal to me, if I recognize them,
But they require, on my part, no act.

Meaning: We do not *suffer* fear, guilt, compassion, shame . . .
                (add here the whole long, terrible,
                (list

We *Invent* these things!

And these inventions are the enemy,
As muscles can be enemy to the leap . . .

(If only I could really understand this)

                McClure says I don't understand this
                Because I use the word "invention" wrong.

Let us see.

      • • • • • • • • • • • • •

A TALE TOLD AS TRUE
    3 people went walking in Golden Gate Park
    among: bulldozers, baseball teams, flowers,   *an*
    & groves. Passing a greenhouse being built   *entertainment*
    they entered a hidden valley, very small,
    where paths wound seemingly untended.
    Unintended.

A TRUE TALE

I held her hand while her brother,
younger than we, ran up and down the *a true tale.*
hillsides *note that as*
inspecting bark, leaves, colors, *we become*
mosses, and rocks both natural and *particular, the*
made by man. *language sinks.*

A PROPHECY, AN EXPLANATION

He will be an artist.
He says he can't decide whether it'll be
poetry or painting, but believes it'll *note how*
probably be painting. Right now he's in *explanations*
the stage where he touches everything *make the*
and eats it. *language stop*
sinking.

He is gathering facts for his art.

ENTRY INTO THE SUNKEN GARDEN

We came to a sunken garden, a
dancing floor, a meeting place, a place *the beginning*
with stones in mystical arrangement, *of invention,*
oaks, shamrocks strangely purple on the *though all*
underleaf. We were hushed. *named things*
are there,
Around us, on the slopes, *kickable*
were fern trees.

INSPECTION OF THE FERN TREES

Strange large Bush-Tree!
Unbelievably ancient form!

(Ancientness. In what sense can I *see* it?)

1. Sober hallucinations on beaches, *at last*
sandy paths and hot trails, *the garden*
together with many dreams, convince me *really sinks!*

Once, in another life, I was
eaten by giant lizards.

2. In Chicago, in a museum, I saw a
   plaster reconstruction of a
   prehistoric fern forest.

3. Familiar with modern forests, I
   see that this ain't like that.

SO!

A prehistoric giant fern forest now GROWING!

(before my very eyes!)

The language is now bent enough I can tell you of the Laurels

---

SIGNIFICANT DETAIL (GROWING, ALSO, BY THE SUNKEN GARDEN)

A grove of Laurel.

(they grow whether I look at them or not)

> *Magical tree!*
> *Leaf in my Mother's stew!*   *the*
> *Crown!*   *beginnings*
>   *of*
> *Chew thy leaves to brighten*   *instruction*
> *color in my eyes?*

(and all that sort of thing)
Disappears, instantly, if I
Only look the other way.

If I look the other way I make:
Baseball players, bulldozers, and, later, owls.

---

to become enamoured of our powers is to lose them. At once!

They grow whether I look at them or not.
They grow whether I look at them or not.

If, as I plan, I return to chew these leaves
(imagining all sorts of ordainments)
I cannot wish they grew on the beach at Taraval St.

Our certainties, our knowledges,
Are even tinier thoughts than these!

Exist
Beyond invention!

Here, a giant CRACK occurs — both audible & blinding!

(testing ourselves,
(we return to the city

MARKET STREET

a city crowd at noon on a weekday.
weather sunny.
light breeze blowing skirts. nicely.

though hungry, I decide to walk 30 blocks
home.

I decide to let it all come in!

The shapes!

Deer, if ever found in these numbers, could never
(and remain deer)
assume this range of shape!

Or gesture!

Every gait, every shoulder-set, *INVENTED*
Their very shapes invented

selection long gone, depending
now on hair-do, money,
address,

•

Intruding Vision: Large doe in Idaho canyon leaping
from underbrush — her twin fawns bounding before her.
Shape and stride beyond invention . . .

•

To a girl, quite pretty,
standing in a traffic-island.

I say: *"You can cross the street now.*

(WALK says green neon light in daytime)

She says: *"I'm waiting for someone."*

I say: *"O. K."*

And I walk past Leo's Haberdashery (consider stealing a sign) when
Heroic girl with braided hair walks by

shape Lenore invented but
not her graceful toss of head or
open eyes

And then Lenore herself, dressed as a Tahitian,
comes riding by in a
Cable-Car made (invention on invention on invention) into a
Truck!

PARADE MUSIC!
LEAFLETS!
FESTIVAL!

(I remember now Lenore's been hired by the
(Pacific Festival. A flop. Event invented, promoted, only . . .

Traffic all jammed up.
5-foot Fairy (sunken garden gone) walking as if
led by his belly-button. With him
B Girl/Business Girl (all Calumet City rushing in on pun)

So I jump onto the Cable-Car-Truck (considering it safer) and
talk to Lenore in din of

> RAH TAH TAH
> TAH RAH TUMMY
> TAH!

At this point I found myself beginning to sob.
(I ought to know better than to let it all in)
And when the truck, at 2 miles per hour, turned

I spun off it,
like off the whirly-disc in the fun-house

> OUT!

trying not to weep
trying not to show them . . .

Out onto the quiet part of McAllister Street where
nothing happens.
Trying to get my wits and nerves back into shape again

> A SHAPE!   A SHAPE!   ANY KIND OF SHAPE BEYOND
>
> INVENTION!

And there,
far back in a steep doorway,
in the empty, sunlit, street
I saw a figure:

> 34 year old (my age) Negro.
> vigorous male body. strong.
>
> he was sitting tight (hiding)
> in that tiny doorway.
> at his feet was a shoeshine box!

His hand, tense, over his eyes
(hiding)

He was crying!
He was crying!

He was crying!

•   •   •   •

I have come to that place in my life
Where I cannot stand this sort of thing anymore.
I see no reason to.

I shall never take another Poet-Walk
(where you let it all come in) on
Market Street, or any similar street in any
City.

I have seen it. I can do nothing about it. It,
though internal to me, since I recognize it, requires no
act. To live, I remove myself from it

(though it goes on whether I look at it or not).

I seek a better shape, a
shape determined by things beyond invention.

As, a few days after the events recounted,
I made a wish over 34 candles on the
cake of my birth

      (but silently,
      (so as not to disturb the merriment, the
      (love being shown me by my friends:

            I, Leo,
            Oak-leaf on my back,
            Striving to uninvent myself,

            Wish, tonight,
            On my 34 candles,
            For a world where never,
            Through man's invention,

Can a man be made to cry like that.

From gardens below invention,
From groves I cannot wish away,
I blow these candles

OUT!

[1960]

[FIRST YOU MUST LOVE YOUR BODY, IN GAMES,]

First you must love your body, in games,
in wild places, in bodies of others

Then you must enter the world of men and
learn all worldly ways. You must sicken.

Then you must return to your mother and
notice how quiet the house is

Then return to the world that is
not Man

        that you may finally walk in the
world of Man, speaking.

PAWN TO QUEEN 4

I am now sitting in my new rustic studio
I haven't had a single vision for 3 months (or more).
My head is full of chess problems.

> There are no excuses.
> "Justify" has become (or should be limited to)
> > a term used by printers.

Still,

THIS LIFE IS NOT SATISFACTORY!

Pawn to queen 4 what?

> Would it please all those who
> love me and believe in my
> absurdly rich gifts, to know it
> has all come to

THIS   ?

> > *This feeble move is all he has,*
> > *for if BQ4, then KTXP ch.*
> > *QXB, PXQ, RXR and white's*
> > *centre has collapsed. Whilst*
> > *if . . . . . .*

It does not even distress me — at least
NOT in that fine old way that used to
FRIGHTEN me (let's face it it was only that)
Into imagining vast projects of beauty and
WORTH. Some few of same now completed & forever
THERE: clumsy lumps in the living rooms of the
young.

Recalling Tzardov's brilliant Q&R
sacrifice, Baden 1924 — an
irrefutable line which has virtually
removed this opening from tournament
play.

Or, to return above, would it be better to fake a
        ". . . gladness, as remote from ecstasy as
        it is from fear"

                    (?)

Impossible evasion !

                BK2 was called for, but the
                text bends under time pressures —
                clearly exhibited by white's
                next move: ignoring QXR and
                mate in 3! However . . . . . .

Pawn (now) to Queen 4 or
Gift?   some
Still remaining sense of duty (?), a desire to make
Report (at least) of a trip taken in (for the most part)
Good health, eyes keen, mind capable of simple
Orderings, a sense of balance unimpaired & not
ONCE

        (a) in jail
        (b) nut house
        (c) Alabama

There ought to be something . . .

                Black finally opens the
                Bishop's file, but the game
                is lost!

                [1962?]

"EVERYBODY CALLS ME TRICKY, BUT MY REAL NAME'S MR. EARL" : A SERMON

Those who live in the world of words kill us who seek
Union with
What goes on whether we look at it or not.

They kill us literally by sending us off to wars with their causes.
They kill us almost literally by sending us to their prisons.
Whose doors are locked & unlocked only by words.
Or fear of their wordy (but very painful) power can
Embitter us into forced silence.

> To become snide is to admit your death.
> The wittily bored are defeated.

For the true state of living things is joy. The
Union always joyful and wild — a thing
Outrageous to the world of words: beyond all law and order.

This is why the true rebel never advertises it, preferring his joy to
Missionary work.
And yet he must speak!

[1963?]

ORANGE TAKE

I've destroyed my brain, part of it,
deliberately, partly, partly, with
booze with age with carbon monoxide (inadvertently,
in Fishing Boat) with city-din with
bachelor food with fasting. Corn Flakes.

Not what it once was. Deliberately.
Some of it gone. All right.

"There's plenty more where that came from"

        (My 22-year-old
          burning of all my poems.
          All right;
          I remembered all but the
          parts that didn't work.
          & rewrote
          Them.

       I am a cliff, from which,
       each day, a
       clod rolls down — a boulder, sometimes,
       in a rained-on road

Or as

I

think of It

An Orange: rotting, but
Rotting from the outside, in, the
Skin of it sluffing away

The skin bitter, anyway.
Red-scale scattered in the pores despite all spraying:

    (inside, bleeds sweetness

[1963?]

IN & OUT, IN & OUT

for M.M.

There she goes again, back to the
Sea she came from:

                        sea-foam tickling at her ass (a bit on the
                        dumpy side — that soft and awful pink!)

It's color of a fat carp rolling in feculent spawning bed or
Recoiling orange Mussel-meat: bright dying
Mucus on a tide rock, the
Shell crushed . . . Harlow's
Busted kidneys

Going again. Out!

                        pink arms over her head, jump
                        to avoid the cold of a wave-slap, then
                        squatting to her neck in it,
                        plunging of her face in it,
                        rising all astream with it . . .

I cannot see her face but know her
Shocked laugh, gasp and tingle, just before her
Flat, free, dive at the
Big next wave

She's gone! Back to the sea she came from
Beautiful! How beautiful it always

Comes and goes!

[1963?]

192

[THREE SONGS IN RAT FLAT]

[1] WITHOUT A RIFLE, ON A CLOUDY DAY

Big lumpy boulder 'cross the canyon
all soft moss

        field

        vert

Dexter: big black bear

        rampant!

[2] SHASTA!

Old mountain,
how many years ago did you spit fire forth molten
rock & gold
splash hills with it, char trees,
incinerate?

        that now you stand so cold,
so huge,
so wreathed in burning cloud, so
burned by setting sun on
mist on

        Rising out of Snow!

that all I can say is Shasta!
I cry Shasta I cry

        Shasta!

[3] BUDDHIST BARD TURNS RAT SLAYER

"Kill, Kill, Kill" Shrieks Wordsmith

I cannot stand your scratch your
nervous skitter twitch of
nose poking through eave-holes scamper
stop scamper over rafters in
dim light of kerosene can't
sleep and it just isn't
cute anymore your

> walnuts, tinfoil,
> maple leaves, your
> shaving brush, you

RAN OVER MY FACE!

> I don't know about dogs but
> rats ain't got no Buddha nature

> DIE!

> DIE!

and found one in my trap: immaculate
gray fur, white breast, white
little paws, short tail, mountain-sweet as
everything else is here

> (all the others died by
> poison

The Cabin

> almost too quiet

ever since

"Rat Flat" is the name I gave to a beautiful cabin I found this winter in the mountains of northern California. An old Wobbly named Lawrence Meyer built the cabin entirely out of material from the woods : Shakes (big shingles) hand-split from Sugar Pine, natural poles for braces, doors of hewn Oak. The interior weathered a uniform golden color, and on a sunny day, or when I lit my kerosene lamp, it was like living in a Vermeer.

These poems are further dedicated to Lawrence Meyer, then, whose ghost led me eerily to his place at a time of great need, and who knew what it meant: "Shaped as wood can be when a man has had his hand to it."

LW

[WHAT A THING TO KNOW!]

What a thing to know!
            Already I'm immortal!

Borrowed Meat will hear what
Chance Meat Sang.

That You will hear, will find,
Mind again,

O Youth!

Who feared Yourself,

                    so much alone!

                        [1964]

DANE POEM

            Until all women start to look like you, are
                        suddenly beautiful as they
                are, were, I dared not let them be

        Danes!
        Boatloads of them brought to my Rome eye!

            (and every one of them knows it

                    like a smell)

                        [1964]

GRAFFITI

Graffiti
of the world unite
the world

write
on every wall in sight

fuck shit piss screw
I love you

Big heart
pierced thru
by an arrow.

People who write on shithouse walls
roll their shit in little balls
People who read these words of wit
end up eating those balls of shit.

Here I sit all broken hearted
Came to shit and only farted

Five feet nine
One seventy pounds
Nine-inch cock
Make date
Make date

Graffiti
of the world unite
the world

write
on every wall in sight

fuck shit piss screw
I love you

Big heart
pierced thru
by an arrow.

Tina and Eddie are
true lovers
and always be.

GRAFFITI

SMALL TURNED ON SONG

Small Ping Pong,
Small turned on song

Ping Pong
Small turned on song

Ping Pong
Small turned on
Song that I love to sing

    Well I read the Saturday
    Evening Post

    Everything I read there I
    Believe there, I believe it's the
    most!

    Post Toasties!

Small Ping Pong,
Small turned on song

Ping Pong,
Small turned on song

    (six bar rest & freak)

NOT READY FOR ME

Magda & Lew

(the Hippy Chick's lament)

I find you not ready for me
Oh please hurry up and catch me.
I find you too late and too slow,
Oh baby come on, let's go!

> It's not very hard,
> It's easy to do,
> Begin with your heart, feel one thing that's true

I find you not ready for me,
Oh please hurry up and catch me.

I find you too late and too slow,
Oh baby come on let's go!

> It's easy to do if you only try
> A wave of your hand, to all that goodbye

Then start in to run as fast as you can
Soon we will fly, be together and then

> Just like the birds we'll start in to sing

I find you not ready for me,
Oh please hurry up and catch me.

[1966?]

SMALL BOOK TO BREAK THE BRAIN

or

(How to Give Yourself Away)

(Being all the Leo Poems and all the Sermons
and commentaries by the Red Monk, up to now.)

All Characters in this book are fictitious. The author invented them
for the sole purpose of exterminating himself, knowing that suicide
is illegal, in every sense and State, but knowing, also, that what we
think of as "Self" is our chief enemy, and must be destroyed. This
creature, which actually does not exist, is very dangerous. It cannot
be killed by a gun, by knife, by bridge-leap, or by meekly turning
itself over to whatever, outside, enemy.

Poor Hart Crane! Mayakovsky!
6,000,000 Jews!
Me!

Missing the whole point by
less than a single step (to
one side or the other)

A VERY IMPORTANT LETTER

"I just can't figure it out. But I think
the problem is in my mind, now, and only
there. I've looked everywhere else and it
certainly isn't to be found anywhere.

"I'm going to sit beneath that tree and
use my mind to find my mind, even if it
means I crush my mind.

"I know of no other way. Goodbye."

Gautama

Commentary by the Red Monk:

*It only took him 9 days and nights. You can't
imagine how relieved he was, for he was very troubled. Not
as you and I are, because all the World was his, by birth,
and he already loved himself, the way he was. He had
learned, at great cost, that he, himself, was perfect, and the
world was something no one in his right mind would want
to own, that the world itself was perfect. Then why was he so
troubled?*

*Remember, also, that those 9 days were the
end of many many years of work. If you shatter a jar
which never had anything in it, what could possibly spill
out?*

LEO'S POET-PLIGHT

1.

Perfectly reasonable demands kill the voice, I'm
irritated beyond all usefulness
                (neither here nor there)
totally immune to Miracle: Union with
what-goes-on-whether-I-look-at-it-or-not.

Or say: "One is possessed with Poetry."
"A gift!"
And suddenly we're stuck with another possession,

the voice is gone.

2.

No use blaming it on clocks to be repaired,
the nuisances of taxes, tickets, money or
the need she has RIGHT NOW for
"the tale that she told of a harsh reproof" —
though they find him, always, caught in
subtlest passages or simply
trying to tune up.

The family learns to get out of the way,
why can't I learn that?
           (or maybe they don't learn it, just
              recognize it, put up with it —
              he's not there anyway & probably
              nowhere else)

You came to me from out of nowhere

(song to the Buddha?)

3.

William Blake was called to dinner and
sat down to a table perfectly set with
empty plates. "These plates are empty!"
"I told you, Mr. Blake, we have no money."

Several humiliating days, all over London,
begging, haggling, no doubt screaming in his heart:

THE VISION!

THE VISION!

Perfectly reasonable demands kill his voice . . .
. . . stuck with another possession . . .

HOW CAN I LEARN TO GET OUT OF MY WAY?

>*the Steig cartoon: a man*
>*wrapped in rope from ankle to*
>*throat, the end of the rope*
>in his teeth . . .

or the question only a German could ask:

>*How can you try not to try?*

Commentary by the Red Monk:

>*Who ever wanted to get out of his way?*
>*Ask* him.

LEO GIVES HIMSELF YET ANOTHER NAME

"I'm the Buddha known as
the quitter." — Jack Kerouac*

I am the Buddha known as *The Beginner.*
Deep in Zazen, *"The Beginner"* (the words)
hit me, simultaneously, in these four ways:
1) Instigator. Inventor.

2) He who is chosen to start, but cannot
finish, as on a relay team, in track.
Once, after passing the baton, I crossed
in front of another team, and my team
was disqualified, though we actually won,
and would have won whether I crossed over
or not.

3) Eternal novice.

4) He who is doomed to begin again and again
and again.

Commentary by the Red Monk:

   In the first place, it was I, not you, who crossed over in front
of another team. This is how we learned right conduct. *Remember,*
instead, how fast we were, and are.
   In the second place, "doomed" is wrong. Avalokiteshvara called
it "returning." When "doom" dies in your mind, "beginning" will
cease to be painful. Avalokiteshvara chose to begin again and again,
though he didn't have to. You said that yourself, in one of your poems.
Don't you believe your own poems?

* Jack said this in *Dharma Bums* to explain to Japhy Ryder, who is, as
everyone knows, Jack's imagined Gary Snyder. Gary had asked Jack to
wash the dishes, or at least help a little with the work around the shack.

LEWIE, YOU'RE A GODDAM JEWEL

We are the grit in the
          clam of this nation   naturally

It tries to slime us

          over.

DOCTOR, CAN YOU SPELL NEBUCHADNEZZAR WITHOUT ANY Z? *

A turf and a clod spells "Nebuchad"

A knife and a razor spells "Nebuchadnezzar"

Two silver spoons and a gold ring
Spells Nebuchadnezzar, the King

* Overheard from the mouth of a senile old Irish lady, on her deathbed.

ACEDIA

for Sister Mary Norbert, O.P.

•

The disease (dis-ease) we call
Acedia, if I am right, was named by Benedict.
Isolated, first, by him, it was
he who saw the symptoms and
offered us a cure.

> I learned the word from Eliot.
> He suffered from it all his life and
> rightly saw the *Spleen* of Baudelaire,
> Acedia:

>> "the result of an unsuccessful
>> spiritual life."

•

"It should be pronounced 'Ah — *Thadia*'
(the girl from Argentina said)
it's Castilian."

> this, because
> it isn't in my dictionary

•

"Sin of the Monks," St. Benedict has it.

And it *is* a strange disease,
caught by none
except the ones of us who try too hard,

> pray too much and
> work too little

>> (with body)

•

THAT was his cure:

Out to the fields (before Matins), at a run.
Back to the Chapel (at a run) for Matins.
Back to the grapes (at a run)

> hard work
> for the body
>
> frees the soul

> •

"Where body is not bruised to pleasure soul"

"Else a great prince in prison lies"

"Wash your bowls!"

> (and countless other confirmations)

> •

Or how we all *do* know it,
in our different ways;
Body   Soul   Mind

> "Ski-tired," I used to call it, or
> "Swimming-tired" . . .

> •

That absolutely Ultimate,
Earned,
Lethargy!

God knows after

any day!

> •

MAITREYA POEM

Ron Loewinsohn: *Why is it whenever*
I see a statue of Maitreya,
he's always laughing?

Phil Whalen: *Maybe it's because he's*
not even here yet, and he's
already made it.

•

At last, in America,
Maitreya, the coming Buddha
will be our leader, and,
at last, will not be powerful, and
will not be alone

> (powerful, but not as Kings are,
> as Johnson tried to be —
> who wielded power more than
> any other king and,
> like the rest,
> wielded it wrong)

How perfect!
The last (first?) Emperor of America
a Texas Millionaire!

•

"and will not be alone" means

> *Each one is one.*
> *There are many of them.*

(Gertrude Stein)

Many.
Many many women and men of such a size
they knew what Patchen meant:

> *it would take little to be free.*
> *that no man live at the expense of another.*

>> (and this is NOT that same old
>> "Second Coming" poem,

>> though that story, too, comes out of
>> what source writes me now)

Take it as a simple prophecy.

•

Look into the cleared eyes of so many thousands,
young, and think:

> *Maybe that one?*
> *That one?*
> *That one?*

And then think:

> *How can they bear it?*

(and vow, as I have, to help them in any way you can)

> *Slouching*
> *toward Bethlehem*
> *to be born.*

•

Look out. (The secret is looking Out.)

And, never forgetting there are
phoney ones, and lost ones, and foolish ones,
know this:

Maitreya walks our streets right now.
(each one is one. There are many of them.)

Look out. For him, for
her, for
them, for

these will break America as
Christ cracked Rome

           (and just tonight
              another one

                  got born!)

[1967]

HOW TO GIVE YOURSELF AWAY

Sermon delivered at Glide Memorial Church
February 25, 1967

THE SERMON OF GLADNESS

The temptation in this wild Age is to
live more wildly (even than that)
because all
things strike so wildly out at us and
baffle so, right now

But "out of your head" means (simply):

> NOT INSIDE THERE, BURROWING
> AROUND, FOR A CHANGE.

(or say it, THE WAY OUT, IS *OUT.*)

                    •

They called it *Compassion* years ago. Rightly.
But then a host of Germans, good men, like Freud
contended that *Compassion* (the capacity for
deep love and care for that which is not YOU)
was really very selfish.

> *SELF-ish*   *Sell-FISH*

and it all got very worrisome, and lonely.
The flower of our HUMAN-being (the need to
get out of ourSELF) withered in
dry fields of SELF-suspicion,

                    But could not stop that

need to bloom.

                    •

Therefore, strange blossoms.
Burnt-out brains.
Endless tapestries of
What was seen at Cactus-time,

Methedrine
Mad houses,

Movies cast on walls being looked upon by
movie-makers casting dreams upon the walls,

> *Old Plato said the loveless world's a cave.*
> *He saw us seated in a smoky light,*
> *staring at a blackened wall where flames gave*
> *images from out a world not real nor right.*
>
> *He said that, outside, sunburnt bodies and*
> *a ceaseless blaze would greet the hardy few*
> *who, by Philosophy, had learned to stand*
> *the glare. And thus he ruled out me and you.*

The rest of the sonnet (the "rest" of it) goes:

> *Come, Barbara, take my hand.*
> *We'll lead us to that sun!*

•

Or, put it this way:

The cave of the mind is the
cave of the mind, and we
seek the opening,
the way out.

And the way out is simply that:
Out.

Compassion. The Flower.

The Flower of this, our Human being, is
Out.

The door of the cave. Compassion.

We turn our back to the blackened wall.

We do not want our recognizable shadows cast upon the blackened wall.

We turn our backs to it.

We take the hand of our beloved and say:
"I cannot go it alone."

And our beloved will take our hand and we will simply walk away. But it will mostly be done in twos.

And this is not even "I and Thou."

It is simpler than that.

•

We have looked too long upon reflections of the Light.

No, not even reflections! More nearly shadows of our *Selves*. The light BEHIND us. The image cast upon the Wall is still *ourSELF.*

We say, "Look, honey, that's me!" Then we wave our hand and, sure enough, the shadow on the wall moves too.

Simply proving that the light is behind us, that we are not standing in its glare.

We look at shadows of ourselves.
Check it out. Does it often flicker, go dim or out, get far too large or blur?

•

Because Love, itself, can never free us.
It only gives us intimations of another Self as
wild as what we made ourself seem to be

staring at the blackened wall

And drugs can never free us.
Can only give us intimations of universes
(still inside, you understand, as dreams are)
similar, but different, from the way we invented it
so many years ago.

"Out of your Mind" means:
Not inside there burrowing about
for a change.

And forcing a wildness may be very brave:
a chinning of yourself upon a half-inch ledge
of rock on the cliff's edge,
but the Void is somewhere else.

Nearer to that bone of
UNinvention which we seek

•

Even further, *SELF* itself is a
rare and beautiful thing,
perhaps known only to those who first had
Human being
  (and then learned how to give himself away).

•

Love can never free us, is only the
natural state we live in as soon as we
give ourselves away.

Drugs will never free us, are only ways to
find the intimations of
how it is to give ourselves away.

And all Temptations, in this wild age,
to live more wildly (even than this)
are only that: temptations.

.

The need is for plain-ness.
To live more plainly (even than this)

And all invention is in vain, or (better)
simple vanity.

.

What we seek is
closer to the bone of
*un*invention

UN . . . invention

Vision we're in terror to let us see —

(allowing all the rest: the others who are not us,
the need to take ahold of some loved hand,
                                        the
joyful knowledge that we seldom find the door alone.)

BUT IT IS THERE!

IT IS THERE!

(The flames, behind us, are not
the Light — the light is out   *THERE*

IT IS WHERE THE LIGHT COMES FROM THAT CASTS
OUR SHAPES UPON THAT BLACKENED WALL

                    •

We take ahold of someone's hand.
We turn forever from those flickering images
            cast upon that blackened wall.

We walk toward the open mouth, the
door, the way, the
ragged circle,
Light, and say:

"Come Barbara, take my hand!
We'll lead us to that Sun . . . . ."

Once outside, we find it:

                    A Gladness as
                    remote from Ecstasy
                    as it is from
                    fear.

[POSTGRADUATE COURSES]

LAW

He who chooses for the chicken
gives bounty for the Bob-Cat

COMPORTMENT

Think Jew
Dance nigger
Dress and drive Oakie

[*1968?]*

A POEM FOR GERARD MALANGA

More people know you
than you know.

Fame.

[1970]

[PREPOSITIONS]

I

In on around about
over through among

beside

under against
over again

out

after

backwards

II

Throughout
furthermore

Moreover and
Nevertheless

III

Beyond

[1970?]

I SOMETIMES TALK TO KEROUAC WHEN I DRIVE

Jack?

Yesterday I thought of something
I never had a chance to tell you
and now I don't know what it was

Remember?

DEAR JOANNE,

Last night Magda dreamed that she,
you, Jack, and I were driving around
Italy.

We parked in Florence and left
our dog to guard the car.

She was worried because he
doesn't understand Italian.

                          Lew

                              [1970?]

CEMENT

Author's Preface

All of my previous books were structured so that each poem nourished, and was nourished by, the others. This book is not like that. It is a wasted field in which, like blocks of cement, the wreckage of my mind is scattered. If you kick any of these poems you, like Sam Johnson, will break your toe. I, like Bishop Berkeley, will insist that that doesn't prove anything at all.

Salt Lake City
May 18, 1970

OUR LADY OF REFUSED LOVE

Sometimes Margaret's mind,

while she sipped a single brandy
or stitched after dinner on a dress she'd bought,

would drift on back through
all of Life and Time

since first our cells slid mindlessly
in hot

and ancient Seas,

and then, before her inner eye, it soon began
to writhe and crawl upon the land

take to the trees and up on out of them
or live in them and
climb back down again, dully

staring at a broken stick and a
sharpened piece of stone,

until attention fixed at last upon the complicated
liquor
the needlework
her fingers, hands, her thighs her
walls

wherein she lived a clean strong life

alone

•

[4/6/70]

The figure of Margaret came from a waitress in a Wisconsin resort, a young girl of such strong beauty I bewailed the vision I had of her certain loneliness. No man could stand against her strident health, her total ability to love if loved enough in return.

Originally the poem was to be the final paragraph (sentence) in a short story where Margaret, the virgin at the resort, got laid young, then became a nurse in World War II, fell in love with a crazy army psychiatrist, returned to the U.S. (after seeing her love for the doctor fail) and then fell in love with a real freak of a civilian doctor, and finally, now nearing 40, had resigned herself to a lonely, but productive, nursing life.

There was a passage in the story where the author speculated on the excellence of Margaret in pioneer days whereas today she is too powerful to be useful.

I never wrote that story and I'm glad.

•

WHALEN'S FEET

One day Philip Whalen and I were walking down Howard Street, near 4th, in San Francisco, and Philip had to take a piss. I wasn't drinking then, or at least not that early, so I stayed outside on the corner, in the sunshine, until he returned.

This is how he greeted me:

"I hate to piss in skid-row bars, the floors are always wet and I have holes in my shoes."

SMALL SENTENCE TO DRIVE YOURSELF SANE

The next time you are doing something absolutely ordinary,
or even better

the next time you are doing something absolutely *necessary,*
such as pissing, or making love, or shaving, or washing the dishes
or the baby or yourself or the room, say to yourself:

"So it's all come to this!"

•

DREAM POEM / MOTHER

Through the years of her speech
a persistent gong
told us how grief had
cracked the bell of her soul.

Dreamed one afternoon and
recovered, almost intact,
after a half hour of not
quite waking up.

•

GETTING BALD

I'm going to wear my hair
as long as I can
as long as I can.

•

MUSTACHE

If you have a mustache,
don't lick it

you'll get cold sores

if you fall, or even get hit

you'll bite your tongue

•

A MEMORABLE FANCY

(Our Lord of Refused Love)

On a cold day in Oregon
in a lightly falling snow

with a 3-day growth of beard
in my hooded parka

I met a man with a sandwich board
proclaiming the coming of the Lord

and I walked around the block
giving him his second chance

to know me.

[7/9/57]

Commentary by The Red Monk

The arrogance of both these people is appalling. The one is making an announcement of hope. The other is making an offering. What can we do to stifle such bad conduct?

INFLATION

for Neil Davis, Innkeeper

At 50 cents
I can buy my second drink
with change from the first.

At 60 cents
I have to wait for my third drink
before I can buy it
with change from the first two.

At 70 cents
I have to wait for the fourth drink
before I can buy it with change.

You have left me penniless,
and drunk.

[1970]

FROZEN PIGEONS

I was young in Chicago when the
gargoyles of
Cement University dripped
beards of ice.
They boarded up the fountains
from the cold.

        It was new to me, Three days of
        hoarfrost was winter on *my* coast.

All frozen and silent, students
scurrying in World War II surplus
jackets and boots, the

whole world turned over:
the poor and the *married*
studying!

        A bad winter.
birds, even,
dropped from those fake
medieval eaves:

frozen pigeons!

They were there, on the ground!
The Feathered People, the
Warm Ones,

Dead!

In that steady cold.

        They boarded up the fountains

        from that cold.

•

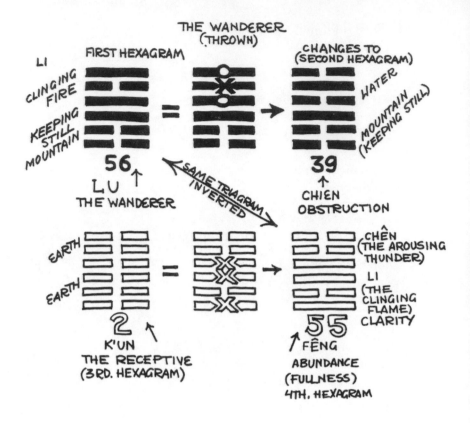

THE WANDERER
(THROWN)

LI
CLINGING FIRE
KEEPING STILL MOUNTAIN

FIRST HEXAGRAM

=

CHANGES TO
(SECOND HEXAGRAM)

WATER

MOUNTAIN
(KEEPING STILL)

56↑
LU
THE WANDERER

SAME TRIAGRAM INVERTED

39
↑
CHIEN
OBSTRUCTION

EARTH
EARTH

=

2↑
K'UN
THE RECEPTIVE
(3 RD. HEXAGRAM)

CHÊN
(THE AROUSING THUNDER)

LI
(THE CLINGING FLAME)
CLARITY

↑55
FÊNG
ABUNDANCE
(FULLNESS)
4TH. HEXAGRAM

THE WANDERER

There was fire on the mountain,
and, seeking to put it out,
he chose to move to the right —
an *Easterly* direction, against
all Nature (for he had not
noticed that the Sun, his sign,
moves *Westerly* — and that all
Men follow the Sun.

Thus the Wanderer walked
all the 64 spokes of the
Great Wheel — of course,
he was fortunate enough,
or fool enough, to have
lept over many of the
Stations of The Way.

How strange to think
that if only he had
chosen to move to his
left on the Great Wheel, or
Westerly, following the Sun,
his wandering would have
ended in a single step —
his present abundance
almost instantly known.

Perhaps he was only born
upside down, or with his
eyes turned in the wrong
direction, or crossed or
something. Who knows?

It's enough to be home,
at last, Magda, for
when you found me I
wasn't even wandering
anymore, just lost —

Abundance, fullness, right
before my eyes. You showed
it to me.

Forgive me for being so stupid,
for taking so much time,
to see.

[October? 1970]

A STATEMENT OF POETICS

LANGUAGE IS SPEECH

Originally published in an eclectic edition titled How I Work As A Poet *(Grey Fox, 1983), this text was the beginning of a textbook for a course in poetry; it grew out of Welch's experiences teaching the University of California Extension Poetry Workshop between 1965 and 1970.*

Preface

Since 1965 I have been teaching a class for the University of California Extension called Poetry Workshop 819. There is no credit for the course and it is open to all. This year, 1970, my course was dropped for budgetary reasons, and I miss teaching it so badly I decided to write a written form of the course. I say "write a written form of the course" because the course itself could never be transcribed since its nature is oral and dependent upon the kind of students who happen to take it.

I always try to have a working writer as a guest for at least one meeting (we used to meet ten Tuesday nights for two hours) and once Allen Ginsberg was the one. I barked for one hour (Allen surprised and delighted me by dropping in unannounced so I just kept on going with whatever I was talking about) and after the break Allen gave a beautiful talk about and demonstration of chanting.

After the class, over drinks, I told Allen I had become a little concerned about the form of the class that gradually over the five years it had distilled into a loose, rambling, skip-about thing that was really a course in Lew Welch, 1A. "Of course," he said, "all they want is to see and hear a live poet. Where else can they find one?"

•

That is one way of going at it. Another way is to think of what language is from the long historical building of it.

In America we speak and write American English, which is completely different from British English, and it all comes from the Sanskrit, we are told, but we learned it from our parents and our friends. It is all we have. Our native speech.

Of course there are other speeches we have, from reading. We have Walpole saying: "I write to relieve, not the emptiness of my purse, but the fullness of my mind." it is almost impossible to read that sentence aloud without going into a British accent.

American English has sentences in it like Burroughs': "Motel,

motel, motel loneliness blows across the continent like foghorns blowing over still oily tidal water rivers."

•

And to know how recent it is! Whitman had no language to write in. There was no American English when he wrote, which is why his poetry seems so awkward at times. For all his rightness and greatness we have to see Whitman as a man fumbling among languages, the British, the French and the emerging American.

•

Language is speech. You ought to be able to say language is speech and then get on with the rest of it, but you can't because so very few believe it.

Language is what goes on when you open the door of a banquet-room and there are 300 ladies having lunch. It is very interesting to hear. It rises and falls, and every once in an inexplicable while it will suddenly stop, there will be a total silence, and then all 300 ladies will hear that silence and comment on it at the same moment. Then you get a roar.

Language is speech. Any other form, the printed one or the taped one, is a translation of language. All poems are translations. This book is a translation of the speech I use when I teach this course, talking to people.

Once I lived in an upstairs room with a single window in it. Outside the window was a large date palm tree. Every sparrow for miles around slept in that palm tree. The din each evening was unbelievable, and it was the same thing every dawn, hundreds of sparrows chattering to each other about where they were to sleep and how it went last night or whatever.

That is language. Speech. The din of a Tribe doing its business. You can't control it, you can't correct it, you can only listen to it and use it as it is.

If you want to write you have to want to build things out of language and in order to do that you have to know, really know in your ear and in your tongue and, later, on the page, that language is speech. But the hard thing is that writing is not talking, so what you have to learn to do is to write as if you were talking, and to do it knowing perfectly well you are not talking, you are writing.

•   •   •

Chapter One

You ought to be able to say "language is speech" and then get on with it, but you can't because so very few people believe it. And if you believe that language is anything other than speech you can't even begin to start knowing what reading and writing is all about.

No one would ever argue that Bach's *music* is the collection of little black notes on paper, but nearly everybody thinks language has something to do with libraries and dictionaries, and that you can "learn" it through the study of good books and grammar. Dictionaries, James Sledd used to say, are the record of usage of people about two generations ago. The street writes dictionaries, the able lexicographer is a recorder and statistician with a fine ear for the language, the speech of a tribe.

Whatever is written down is a translation of a speech. It cannot become language until it is "played," respoken.

I never used the word "respoken" before. Isn't it nice?

You have to love language to be a reader and a writer, have to have language in a way different from ordinary speakers. You have to have language in a concrete way where the words and the structures are held, not simply as ways to get a thing said, but as a cabinetmaker holds his tools and his wood.

It takes a gift of ear as definitely as music does. You can train the ear, make yourself able to hear yourself hearing without losing what is being said, but if you're born speech-deaf you're as irreclaimable as a tone deaf musician.

Another analogy with music comes to mind. A student at the freshman level of a fine music school had perfect pitch, but was so meter-dumb he couldn't march with the football band even though he was right next to the bass drum. His "music" was very strange. It existed outside of time. He won all kinds of prizes as a kid in some small town but couldn't play *with* anybody else.

Some people are meter-dumb with language. They cannot hear or produce a structure. The words sort of roll along one after the other and miraculously refuse to make any kind of pattern. A good writer should have a good enough ear to hear this phenomenon well enough to transcribe it. Thomas Mann's "Peppercorn." An amazing feat, to hear and handle non-structure.

We'll get into that later, with Gertrude Stein.

And we must digress here in deference to John Cage and Ives. Let's go back to the tone-deaf man and music.

Ives' father was the choirmaster of a small church and led the congregation in the hymns. One of the members was a huge Swede who just loved to sing, who sang very loud, and who never hit one note "right." Other members complained to Mr. Ives, couldn't he somehow make the man be quiet because he was throwing every-body else off? Ives said, "Have you ever looked at that man's eyes when he's singing? Have you ever listened to what he *does*? That man knows more about music than any of you."

Which brings up another fascinating thing. You can have a fine ear, but you can't, maybe, get the note into your throat as the ear hears it. My wife is this way. Magda can hear as well or better than I can, proves this by being able to tune instruments and hi-fi sets better than most people. But she can't "carry a tune." It's very strange to hear her singing in the bathtub. It's like the big Swede: it's all "wrong" but it is *music* far more beautiful and true than all the Judy Garlands and Barbra Streisands in the world.

Some people have a very fine ear for the words of others, but have difficulty bringing their own words to Mind. "Bringing your words to Mind" is the whole thing, too. We'll gradually get to that.

Right now I want to get into an imitation of two hours speak-ing-time as much as possible about language and speech and the ear and different ways we can all go about it.

One of my most beneficial teachers was James R. Sledd, the distinguished structural linguist at the University of Chicago. At Reed College I did my thesis on Gertrude Stein, and that study convinced me that if I were ever to learn about writing I'd have to stop reading and start looking flat at the stuff of writing itself. So I took history of English and structural linguistic courses from Sledd. The man really altered my mind — really showed me the wonders and mysteries of this thing we call language. First of all, he forever removed my prejudices regarding dialect.

Like my wife, Sledd had a wonderful ear but could not, even slightly, mimic any dialect other than his own. He spoke in the broadest, flattest, Georgia-cracker accent imaginable. I was shocked. I was raised in California where you're taught to believe that Okies are inferior, and here I was in graduate school taking linguistics, and Chaucer's English yet, from a Cracker!

Sledd got right into it. "You are probably struck by the way I talk, so let's get it straight right now. I can't mimic. I was always a bright kid and I got a scholarship to Harvard and there I learned you shouldn't say runnin' and jumpin' and kickin', you should say runnING and jumpING and kickING." (And he was a riot saying those words, the "G" sound struck like the natives of Long Island say "Lon Guyland.") "Well," he went on, "one day I came home and smelled this wonderful smell and I said to my wife, *Honey, are we having fried chickING tonight?*, and then I said to myself, *Sledd, you are a fraud.*"

He then gave a marvelously witty lecture about how he had

a good ear but couldn't mimic any other dialect and how it had nothing of importance to do with language other than to indicate how the man's mother and father talked, and how at the end of the course we could hear him try to read Chaucer, a treat.

Language is speech, but speech is not dialect. You can read Faulkner without imitating his Mississippi dialect and you'll lose nothing. Dialect is only a regional and personal voice-print. This is very difficult for many people to believe, but it is so. You can easily separate structure and meaning from dialect, and still be dealing with sound, with the music, with speech, with another's Mind.

Gertrude Stein perfectly mimicked the rhythms and structures of the speech of Baltimore Blacks in her story *Melanctha,* and she didn't transcribe the dialect at all — that is, didn't have to misspell a lot of words to get the work done. Nelson Algren has many many passages with no misspellings, but he catches the real flow of a regional speech.

It took poor Sledd nearly six weeks to rid me of my terrible prejudice. One day I finally heard what the man was doing with language. I heard, really heard, the beautiful structures he made as he talked. He could extemporize a sentence with 20, 30, or even 50 clauses in it and the clarity was blinding.

He freed me also of my stupid idea that there was a right and wrong grammar. There is only grammar. Grammar is the word we use to mean the description of the structure of speech. Period. And we all know our grammar perfectly, otherwise we couldn't be understood. Grammar is the description of the structure of something that's already made, and we know the meaning of an utterance because of the structure, not because of the word-meanings only.

Sledd's example, one of them, was this. Suppose you found a telegram on a man's desk and you don't know the man or anything about him. The telegram reads: *Ship Sails Today.* There is no way to know whether the telegram refers to a ship sailing today, or is a request to ship some sails to some yachtsman. You can't know, because the structure is not given. You make the structure by putting in the *the*. Ship *the* Sails Today, *The* Ship Sails Today.

There are lots of long books about all this and 1A is not a linguistics course, so I don't want to get bogged down here. But here is an example of my own invention which gets us into the neighborhood of what we're saying.

I once was a bus-driver for a private grammar school in Chicago. One of my favorite kids was a boy named Mark in about the 4th grade. I asked him how he was doing and he said he was having a lot of trouble writing because he didn't know what a sentence was.

"I don't know what a sentence is is a sentence," I said.

"Is it?"

"Is it is a sentence."

"It is?"

"It is is a sentence, and so is it is is a sentence."

And so on, playing the game all afternoon. Finally I asked him to say something that was not a sentence. He couldn't do it. "I can't," he said. "I can't is a sentence" said I, and then I told him to put a capital at the beginning of one of those things and a period at the end of it, and to pretend he was talking when he wrote — to talk it first, and then write it down.

Then I said, "You told me a story about your grandmother the other day, let's write it down." He did, and from that paper forward was always the best writer in his class.

This part of it is so simple only true readers and writers and language-lovers can understand it. It is all ear, it is all already understood, it is all totally mysterious.

Language is as much a part of having Human being as anybody's left leg or liver. It's totally organic. You can't change it, correct it, or get along without using it. When Trappists and others take vows of silence they are really taking on something. The spiritual intensity which results must be terrifying, and my guess is few non-speakers do more than withdraw. Try it, for even a day or two.

In the Zen koan: You are bound hand and foot and are hanging by your teeth from the branch of a tree which is leaning out over the void. Rats are nibbling at the roots of the tree. Somebody comes by and says *What is Zen?* You must speak. What do you say?

Must speak always struck me as meaning *being human, you must.*

Once Whalen ended a letter with: *I speak as clearly as possible considering that my mouth is full.*

•

I don't know the answer to that koan but I do see this thing we call language as an inexhaustible delight and wonder. It constantly comes out of the mouths of the people, a vast din which will not stop. Its origin is lost. Its changes are unexplainable. Its structures are indescribable.

Somewhere about two or three years old we begin talking in what is called a sentence. No linguist has been able to come up with a general description of what a sentence is. Yet everybody knows what it is, as we saw in the case of Mark.

There is a beautiful set of books by Jespersen which begins with the sentence *Birds fly* and which keeps at it for several volumes until you get to things like *In Italy where the thermal currents are such that swallows and other cliff-dwelling denizens are unable to maintain purchase, the birds, while seeking shelter and food, fly no less rapidly than their English counterparts.* (I just made that one up now in haste, Jespersen's building is far more interesting.) And when he was through he had gotten nowhere near an adequate description or analysis of the English sentence.

Anyone could get a Ph.D. thesis, at once, if he could do this — be the paper less than one page long.

Add to this mystery the inexplicable changes you can trace through even a cursory study of the history of English or any other language, and you do see language as a huge growth handy for our use but forever beyond our ken.

Nobody knows why the great vowel shift occurred in English. Nobody knows why love used to rhyme with prove but no longer does. Nobody knows why the distinction between shall and will is no longer important to us. And the subjunctive is definitely disappearing as many of the old *do* forms did.

It is enough to know *that* these things happened and are happening and always will go on happening. We humbly listen to the din of the Tribe and balance ourselves on the edge of it, like a surfer on a huge wave.

Sledd used to get letters from the public like *My son can't seem to learn the proper way to use who and whom.* He answered *Tell your son never to use whom in conversation.* He pointed out to us that when you answer a telephone *To whom am I speaking* you are now saying two things, you are saying *I don't know who is on the other end of this line* and you are also saying *I am a pedant.* If you want to make it known that you are a pedant fine, but if not, not. And there is no way to get out of this bind. Language is final. What is said is said. Whether you like it or not.

•

Intellectually much of the foregoing is baby talk, somewhere around A, B, and C, in the alphabet of Mind. Don't be surprised or ashamed if the simpleness of the clump of observations is hard to believe. I had the very best teachers, was born glib and gifted with an ear for language, and it was years before these things became obvious and delightful, available to ear and speech.

My years of teaching, reading the works of students, their poems and papers, convinces me that starting with this quick *language is speech* business is necessary and helpful.

You can't go wrong with these arguments. At worst you can

get your ear to working, and at best you can throw out all those tortured sentences you used to call a poem.

Based upon all this, but much more interesting, is the whole question of how words come to Mind.

Whatever it is inside there it is certainly, in the beginning, not words. It can come to be words, probably will if the need is real enough, as organically as the steady juicing of the glands, but first of all it is not yet words. How do we bring words to Mind?

I am sitting at my typewriter now bringing out these words to get them off my Mind. I am trying to transmit something, in words. They come out faster or slower and make a pattern, actually many patterns, and it all goes back and forth.

Whalen once said: *The problem is how to get out of my way.*

There are also the problems of whether I am remembering or thinking or making or talking or writing.

●

Once, on the way to Oregon, I stopped at a California winery to get free wine from the tasting room. Just at that time a tour was starting so I decided to go along. A young man of about 23 was the guide and began that strange kind of language guides use, almost a chant: . . . *and on the left a 1500 gallon redwood barrel containing Burgundy kept always at the temperature of* . . . and then he said *Whose kid is that?*

The force of *whose kid is that* caused everyone to pay attention to the real moment we were all in. A small child was about to fall into a very deep vat of wine.

I vowed, at that moment, that every statement in my poems should have at least the force of *whose kid is that.*

It is an impossible standard, but a good one. Few really bad lines can stand against it.

The guide was chanting remembered lines to a vapid audience. The distance between his Mind, our Minds, and the subject of wine-making simply was not being bridged. But the endangered child called words to his Mind which were immediate and un-premeditated — it was organic, as a leap would be if one were frightened by a truck.

●

In "What Are Master-pieces and Why Are There So Few of Them" Gertrude Stein points out that writing deals constantly with the problem of the difference between thinking and remembering. Writing must never be remembering. If it is, it is a confusing bore. But, as Stein points out, thinking and remembering are so nearly the same thing.

Everyone knows the difference between thinking and remembering, some more keenly than others, but all of us really do know that there is a difference. Perhaps the story of the guide in the winery helps.

The guide in the winery, at the moment he said *Whose kid is that,* was using language in an exact relationship with his consciousness. He was trying to get some work done. He spoke without thinking or remembering. He simply spoke. And the people on the tour responded immediately, without thought. The child, thereby, was saved.

Poetry should be at least as intense as this. It very seldom is.

The few poems we prize over the centuries and across all cultures and times are *more* intense than this.

How do we bring words to Mind?

The answer is we bring words to Mind in all sorts of ways for all sorts of purposes and in every degree of intensity and accuracy. Some few bringing of words to Mind we call poems.

How are the words of a poem brought to Mind?

•

When I was Chief Copy Editor of Montgomery Ward and Co. my Job was to check the ads the 45 copywriters under me wrote. They were very simple-minded word structures. *This is a refrigerator. It is big and white. Every time you open the door the light turns on. It keeps things cold. Wards sells refrigerators for less than most folks. Buy now. Save.*

This and similar messages had to be bent into interesting patterns, or at least space-filling patterns, over and over again, about all of the familiar items we have in our homes. There should be information: how big is it? why is it more expensive than the other models? what reason is there to buy it now instead of later?

Even at this mundane a level the art of writing proved so demanding to the copywriters (and many of them were gifted; Sherwood Anderson had precisely this kind of job) that there was a joke among the other employees about the *copywriter's trance.*

It was true. You could go through the seas of desks and spot a working copywriter every time. He or she would be staring straight ahead, perhaps with a half-smile but mostly with a vacant sort of puzzled frown, and then *peck peck peck* on the typewriter, and then another frozen, vacant, trance-like staring at nothing. Then *peck peck peck* again. Occasionally a furious burst.

The trance was respected by the other employees. You waited until the concentration broke, and only then did you ask whatever question you had in mind.

•

The copywriter in his trance is neither thinking nor remembering, though his mind is doing things that partake of both. He is writing. He is bringing words to Mind. He is doing this in an unusual way, that is to say he is doing it in a way we don't ordinarily see him do it in conversation, or while buying cabbages in the market or making change.

He is bringing words to Mind in writing rather than in talking. It is an important difference. It is almost impossible for him to say *Whose kid is that* with the absolute directness of the winery guide. But this directness, or the semblance of it, should, I think, always be his goal.

•

He is in a trance. And all he is trying to do is make his living writing baby-talk ads for a mail-order house.

But Li Po, while extemporizing intricate lines on whatever subject the Emperor happened to throw at him, dropped, I am sure, into the same glazed-eyed stare. His eyes would then clear, and he'd wittily speak his lines.

I saw William Carlos Williams do this on a challenge from Snyder and Whalen and me in 1950.

There is clearly something special about the way we bring words to Mind when we write. We do something different from what we do even when we exactly speak, as the winery guide exactly spoke and saved the child. (Usually, of course, we don't speak with any exactness at all. It is mostly ceremony and blather.)

With any exactness? Exactness to what?

What we try to do in the situation of teaching or writing or confessing or standing firm against those who would cheat us or lie to us or kill us, what we try to do when we need most to speak openly to our beloved or to those who believe in us, need us, ask us for really necessary advice, is to try to be, in words, exact. We must now speak. And we must now be exact. To what?

This is the moment you bring words to Mind as the poet brings words to Mind. It is why we prize poetry, in spite of all the sloppy examples of writing that go under the name of poetry. We all know what we go to poetry for. We want the exact transmission of Mind into Word.

●

We don't care how crazy that man is, we want exact transmission of that crazed Mind. We are crazed ourselves. It would help to know we are not alone. We are delighted by the calmness of this other one. We are sent to the woods to see, really see, what we'd so often looked at and never noticed at all, by that other Mind. We need to know exactly what it must be like to be an ambassador, a killer, a hulking fool.

●

Since the business of living has so many barbs in it, and since so many of our friends are liars or fools or inarticulate or emotionally blunt or are sucking on us for what they imagine we can give though we can't, it is pure joy to read the poems of the truth-sayers, the simple singers, the masters of prayer and devotion, and the crazed, wise, babblers of Ecstacy, the High-Mind Singers to no end.

Exactness? Exactness to what? You know what you want in the writing you read, and you know how seldom you get it. We want exact transmission of Mind, in words (we can get it in dance, occasionally, or music, just as seldom, in painting just as now and then, but in this book we are thinking about writing and reading and so we are talking about words, and how they come to Mind).

●

The words come to Mind through the whole history of whatever Tribe you learned your language in. The words come to Mind through all the private history of how you've lived your Human Being. There is no way to cheat, unless you go to too many schools, and try to be a poet.

Try to be a poet? What a blasphemy!

Unless you mean, as Gregory Corso did when he got the calling in a prison in New York, to use the native speech which is as much a part of you as your eyes and hair, and mean to use it to the end of truth and life (against all odds in a deranged world), to use this speech, your own speech, the language of your father and your mother and your friends, the primary tool of all your actions toward all your wants and needs, to use this speech as a weapon, a tool, a singer's voice, the means to total sharing of all your Mind, unless you mean to do that, then to try to be a poet is a blasphemy.

•

Accuracy. Accuracy to what? Exactness. Exactness to what?

Maybe we ought to say the words *are brought* to Mind, because the more you work with this process the more it seems, as the Muse Idea has it, that the words *come* to Mind, unasked.

I was taking a nap in the afternoon of a hot day in Chicago. I had a dream in which I was reading a very long book, 1500 pages, called *Expediencyitis*. I dreamt it was written by a German, name blurred. The form of the book was the form of this one: blocks of paragraphs divided by centered dots. I was struck, in my dream, by the great wisdom of the book, and eagerly read page after page.

I began to awake.

As I began to awake I had several thoughts. I was sorry the dream was going to come to an end because the book I was reading was so very wise and beautiful. Then I had the thought, while still dreaming, that of course if I was the dreamer then I had written the book, not the blurry German. It was my book. It was what I, if I could only write better, would write. (I was about 26 years old with very few real poems.)

I then dreamed (thought/dreamed) that I'd surely not be able to remember and write down any of those beautiful and profound paragraphs. I was almost awake.

I then thought/dreamed the idea of going back into the dream and capturing some of the text of *Expediencyitis* with the idea of writing it down if I could find some of it. I was successful. I went back into the dream and came back with a single piece from the book.

> Through the years of her speech
> a persistent gong
> told us how grief had
> cracked the bell of her soul.

I wrote this down while still drowsy, and it was three months before I realized that this was a poem about my mother. *Us* is my sister and I, and my mother really had, through the years of her speech, told us of her grief. The *gong, told, bell* (with *cracked* working in there as in the Liberty Bell) are pieces of craft (craft?) totally unavailable to me at the time of this dream, and rarely available to me now.

Imagine what the rest of that book said.

●

Accuracy. Exactness.

We have to be exactly accurate to what we have in Mind. That is all we have.

If we are to make of that Mind in words, then we have to be absolutely accurate in the way we use our native speech, since that, too, is all we have. It is our only language.

The shape of our Mind is the shape of our native speech, since our native speech helped to shape our Mind.

"Mind is shapely." Mind speaks in many ways.

●

"Mind is shapely." Mind speaks in many ways.

Perhaps you are a dancer. Others, as John Cage did, show Mind in the form of music. Finally, John Cage has become a writer, a very accurate and exact one, a true poet of American language, a heavy case in favor of my argument about ear-training.

Or maybe, as my friend Jack Boyce is, you are a painter. He is truly a painter. He is astonished that I can't see things in his paintings which are obvious to him, since I dearly love paintings and know a great deal about looking at them. I am occasionally surprised by his inability to see some nice (nice means precise, but has been misused) thing in a piece of writing. He is a painter, I am a poet.

There are many ways to bring the Thing to Mind.

Now I said the shape of our Mind is the shape of our native speech, since our native speech helped to shape our Mind. But in a more general way we have to realize that I am a word man, that I have *speech* in my vocabulary with a peculiarly heavy emphasis.

Actually the whole thing about the different arts is that they all do the same thing in any place and at any time though they do use different materials.

The reason they do the same thing at any particular place and time, depending on the alertness of a particular art-form as compared to some other one, is that the Mind of a time and place must be One. Mind is always One, but it is always easier to see how that is if you look at a particular place and time. You see how shapely it is.

Our time is just as shapely as any of the others, the 18th Century or the Tang Dynasty or whatever you may choose to see as one-of-a-piece. When you live in a time, as we all must do, it is hard to see it as anything except discordant.

But our time is going along with perfect order, we are all of one Mind, it only is hard to prove it and of course there are a large number of people alive now and in power who are of the Mind of two generations ago. This is always so. Perhaps now it is more dangerous than in previous periods, but the fact is power has always been in the hands of those who live as if the world were what it was two generations before.

Gertrude Stein made the distinction between those who live *in* their generation and those who are *of* their generation. Those *in* their generation are always thinking two generations back, those *of* their generation are *making* the thing as it really is being made. Of course it is not there yet.

It is really an exhilarating thing to be *of* your generation, and especially lately it is scary and important to know that now I am 44 years old and frequently I find myself holding on to something back there in the Beat Generation days and the thing has slid by me, like an ocean wave. There is no saving it. It is over. It is going to be something. It is good to feel yourself as one who helps it along, whatever it may be. And to notice how it is, not as it ought to be, but how it really is. And can you ride it? Can you sing it? Will it, and this is presently a real concern, get too heady for you to handle? The safe ways are now, at 44, becoming far too available.

•

We are still talking about Language as Speech and how that has to do with writing and reading. We got into Mind unavoidably, since after all you do bring the words up out of your Mind, there being no other source. And we became interested in the question of how you do that, how you get what is not words into words (or dance or paint or sculpture or whatever it is you do to make Mind something out there for the others to use, though you have the perfect right to just let it buzz in there for your own joy entirely).

But that never is enough. We are makers. Those of us who are fortunate enough to be able to handle the daily living business and still find time to learn ornate crafts become what the world calls artists. Some of us go straight to being artists without learning how to handle the simple daily tasks. But the happiest men and women in the world are those of us who find that if we don't, actively, make the chores of the day too difficult, there'll be lots of time left for the play we call art. And that if we do that we have the added joy of friends and strangers who love to see or hear or feel what we do, and we have the even greater pleasure of being able to meet, as peers, the other maniacs who live the way we live, and make the way we make. If it were still possible to be a romantic, I would say I have lived my life as if I thought I were a hero, and I know for a fact that all of my dearest friends are heroes and heroines to their toes.

The worst Persian voluptuary could not have dreamed my most ordinary day.

[Early fall 1970]

A BRIEF CHRONOLOGY

1926   Lewis Barrett Welch, Junior, was born in Phoenix,
        Arizona, at 9:40 p.m. on 16 August, the son of
        Dorothy Brownfield Welch and Lewis Barrett Welch.

1929   His mother took Lew and his sister, Virginia, to
        California, and thereafter he seldom saw his father
        before the latter's death in 1947.

1932–40 Attended grammar schools in Coronado, La Mesa,
        and El Cajon in southern California. It was his seventh
        grade teacher, Robert Rideout, who stimulated his
        interest in reading.

1940–44 Attended junior high school and high school in Palo
        Alto, graduating in 1944. In high school he was a
        track star, winning the 400 in 49.7 s.

1944–45 He enlisted in the Army Air Corps when he was 17,
        and in the fall of 1944 he enrolled as a freshman in
        engineering, the University of California at Berkeley.
        In January 1945 he was called to active service in the
        Air Force, and was stationed at Amarillo Army Air
        Field in Texas for basic training, and in April was
        transferred to Lowry Field in Colorado for training as
        a B-29 Remote Control Turret Mechanic Gunner. In
        November he was discharged from active service.

1945–46 Rather than return to college at once, Welch worked
        first in a garage, and then later in a men's haberdashery
        in Palo Alto. In the fall he entered Stockton Junior
        College where he studied English, music and painting.
        Through a teacher, James Wilson, he became
        interested in Gertrude Stein and in writing, and was
        encouraged to complete his college education at Reed
        College.

1948–50 Enrolled at Reed College as a junior with a major in
        English. Here he began to write poetry, and became

friends with Gary Snyder and Philip Whalen; with them he published his first poems in *Janus,* the college literary magazine. He played the part of Balthasar in a revival of *Much Ado About Nothing,* composing the music for his songs. He studied calligraphy under Lloyd Reynolds, and comparative literature with Frank Jones, who directed his B.A. thesis on Gertrude Stein, which was accepted in June, 1950. In late October, with Snyder and Whalen, he met William Carlos Williams when he came to Reed to give a reading. In November he traveled to New York City, visited Williams in Rutherford, continued Stein studies in the New York Public Library, and clerked in Stern's department store.

1951–53   In April he quit his job and traveled to Florida with old Reed College friends for a course of therapy. In the fall he entered graduate school at the University of Chicago, where he first majored in philosophy and then transferred to English. James R. Sledd's course in linguistics was an important experience.

1953–57   He worked as a junior executive in the advertising department of Montgomery Ward & Co.

1957   In October, at his request, he was transferred to the Oakland headquarters of Montgomery Ward, to which he commuted from San Francisco.

1958–59   He lost this job, which he had come to find meaning-less, and began to devote more time to writing. He supported himself by driving a Yellow Cab, and lived at East-West House, an early experiment in commune living. Zen meditation with Gary Snyder in his Mill Valley cabin. "Chicago Poem" was published in *Contact,* and he gave a reading at the Poetry Center of San Francisco State College. In November he and Albert Saijo drove Jack Kerouac to New York; by Christmas he had returned to his mother's home in Reno.

1960   In Reno, inspired by Jack Kerouac's advice and ex-ample, he began work on his novel, *I, Leo.* His poems appeared in *The New American Poetry; Wobbly Rock,* his first book, was published by Auerhahn Press. By summer he had returned to San Francisco where he met Lenore Kandel. In August they drove Jack Kerouac down to Big Sur for a weekend (Lew appears as David Wain in Kerouac's novel, *Big Sur*, and Lenore as Romona Swartz). In November he drove to Portland with Jerry Heiserman and gave a reading at Reed College.

1961   With Kirby Doyle he gave a performance of "The Din Poem" at the Batman Gallery in San Francisco. His story, "The Man Who Played Himself," was published in *Evergreen Review*. He worked in commercial salmon fishing with Bill Yardas and other fishermen.

1962–63   After the fishing failed, and he broke with Lenore, he suffered a severe breakdown. In July he stayed in Lawrence Ferlinghetti's cabin in Big Sur, then he went north to the Trinity Alps country where he had found an abandoned cabin near Forks of Salmon by August. Here he met the painter Jack Boyce, wrote his *Hermit Poems* and drafted the poems of "The Way Back" series. At times he worked on Trail Crew for the Forestry Service. By December he had returned to San Francisco.

1964   Participated with Gary Snyder, just back from Japan, and Philip Whalen in a KPFA "On Bread and Poetry" panel discussion, and in June in the big "Freeway Reading." Worked as a busboy in the Trident restaurant in Sausalito. Met Magda Cregg in July and lived with her in Strawberry and Marin City until February 1971.

1965   Read at the University of British Columbia Arts Festival in February. In the spring, with Robert Duncan, helped organize a show called "Looking at Pictures with Gertrude Stein." Participated in the University of California (Berkeley) Poetry Conference in the summer. *Hermit Poems* published by Four Seasons Foundation, and *On Out* by Oyez/Berkeley.

1965–70   Taught the Poetry Workshop of the University of California Extension in San Francisco. His students included Frank Dietrich, Tony Dingman, Julian Michel and Charles (Skip) Upton. During these years he gave many readings, especially at colleges and universities in the western states. Worked for several years as longshoremen's clerk on the docks of San Francisco.

1966   Gave "One-Man Plays" reading at the San Francisco Museum of Art in October.

1967   In February he delivered a sermon, "How to Give Yourself Away," for the Glide Memorial Church. He played the Cop in Robert Nelson's film *The Great Blondino.*

1968   Published "Greed" and "Final City, Tap City" in the *San Francisco Oracle. Courses* published by Dave Haselwood. In the fall he taught a course in Afro-American literature at the College of Marin. Wrote reviews for the *San Francisco Chronicle.*

1969–70   Read with Richard Brautigan at San Quentin. *The Song Mount Tamalpais Sings* published as Maya Quarto Five. He conducted a "Literary Get-together" course at the Urban School of San Francisco. Completed work on his collected poems, *The Ring of Bone,* and signed a contract with a New York publisher. In June and July of 1970 he was poet in residence at Colorado State College in Greeley.

1971   In January he was invited to Reed College to give a reading and to conduct a writers' workshop for a week. In March he joined Bill Yardas in Vancouver, Washington, and worked on the docks there. On 30 March he returned to Reed to give a lecture on "How I Work as a Poet." In mid-April he returned to San Francisco briefly, and then drove to Gary Snyder's home in Nevada County, where he planned to build a small cabin on Allen Ginsberg's adjoining land, working with a crew during the summer. On 23 May, in a deep depression, he took his revolver and walked away into the forest leaving a farewell note. His body has not been found.

D.A.

INDEX OF TITLES AND FIRST LINES